A RECIPE FOR
RESTAURANT
SUCCESS
Workbook

*Start your Journey Here to Launching **Your Own** Food Establishment*

CHARLES OKWALINGA

ACTION WEALTH PUBLISHING

LONDON- NEW YORK- -DUBAI- -NAIROBI

CONTENTS

UNIT 1

GETTING STARTED

Many people want to open a restaurant. This Workbook will help people from all backgrounds when it comes to opening their restaurant. No matter who has the initial idea, you will find that this Workbook is very helpful when it comes to navigating the complexities of opening your Dream Restaurant.

Opening a restaurant can be a wonderful and challenging experience. For some, opening a restaurant is a dream come true. For others, it represents a new business venture. However you arrive at the decision to open a restaurant, having sound advice when it comes to running one is the main key to success.

What makes a Successful Restaurateur

There are many factors that make a restaurant successful, and there are many factors that make for a successful restaurateur. While the majority of my book *A Recipe for Restaurant Success* and this Workbook explains the elements needed to make a successful restaurant, it is a good idea to spend some time making sure you remember and maintain *the elements that make for a successful restaurant owner.* A restaurant can have the best location or ambiance in a city, but, under bad management, even this restaurant can fail. By following a simple list of personal qualities, you will dramatically increase your chances of success in the business.

- ➤ **A Commitment to Quality**: To become very successful in the restaurant business, you need to build a large and loyal clientele. Having a high commitment to quality greatly increases your chances of success.
- ➤ **Great People Skills:** To make sure you remain close to your clientele, it is important to remain visible to your customers. A restaurant where the owner is present represents a well-run business.
- ➤ **Great Money Management Skills:** Most restaurants run out of money before they have the opportunity to turn a profit. For this reason, all great restaurateurs have great management skills. Before the doors open, you want to make sure you have enough cash on hand to cover the expenses for an entire business year.

> ➢ **Be a Great Organizer:** To understand all the aspects of your business model, you need to be a great organizer. Make sure to actively look for ways to improve your organization on a daily basis. Building a fast and efficient system will allow you to spend more time completing the more enjoyable tasks of the restaurant business

Research, Research, Research

Before you decide to open the cheque book and start a company, you need to conduct tons and tons of research. For a start, it's important to build a map of restaurant competition in your area before you make any significant decisions when it comes to your restaurant concept. For instance, if there are four pizza shops in your desired location, there is no point adding your own version of pizza to the mix. At the same time, you do not want to open a restaurant with a concept that is too specific. Instead, you want to find one which is <u>underserved</u> in your area. Meaning, you need to find a concept that will be popular with the local clientele, but where you cannot find too many other restaurants which also serve this segment.

As of this writing, there are some notable trends worth researching and investigating. These include:

- ✓ **Mixologists and Cocktail Driven Bars:** Fancy and highly involved cocktails are all the rage these days. A mixologist is someone who employs modern techniques to create inventive cocktails.
- ✓ **In-House Soft Drinks:** While Coke and Pepsi have dominated the soft drink business for nearly a century, a new movement has taken off that involves the creation of in-house sodas. Here, the restaurant creates rich and flavoursome syrups, which are then combined with water and carbon dioxide; the recipe is bottled and served to the restaurant crowd. This is a great way to create a unique concept as well as create a retail item to sell in your restaurant.
- ✓ **Premium Quick Service:** Consumers still demand high quality ingredients and creative recipe concoctions. When consumers eat a cheeseburger, they want high quality beef, cheese, bread, and crisps. Consumers are also keen on eating high quality ethnic foods in quick service settings. For this reason, consider opening a premium quick service restaurant.
- ✓ **Artisan Snack Food Shops:** Consumers are looking for meals that are made not only made with organic ingredients but are homemade. In artisan snack food shops, breads are made at the store, crisps are cut from potatoes and fried in the shop and the ketchup is typically a signature recipe from the shop.

- ✓ **Technology-Driven Menus:** Technology is all the rage in restaurants today. A new and emerging trend is to use iPads or other tablets to share menus, place orders, and give the customer a unique user experience.
- ✓ **Nutrition:** The modern consumer requires a healthy meal nowadays. When major chains in the United States were forced to publish the nutrition of their foods on the menu, these companies were surprised when sales for such items reach 40% of total sales. Formulating a nutritionally-minded menu will certainly increase your traffic significantly.
- ✓ **Locally Focused Food:** many restaurants have turned to local sources of ingredients to reduce their carbon footprint. Not only do locally focused menus help the environment, but they also help the local economy by supporting local farmers. Make sure to take time to contact local farmers and farmer's markets.

EXERCISE: YOUR RESTAURANT NICHE

You may have already done this research or may still need to do some in order to complete this exercise. But consider your target restaurant "market": your city or town, your neighborhood, maybe even your county. Drawing an imaginary circle around that target area, look at the restaurants there to answer the first question. What type of food service is there *too much of?* Then, describe the sort of restaurant you have in mind. Include any of the trends mentioned above, if they apply, or new ones that are developing locally. Finally, identify the competition for your new restaurant in that market

What we *don't* need in my target market:

_____
_____
_____
_____
_____
_____
_____
_____
_____
_____
_____
_____

Our restaurant idea:

What would be our competition?

Research, Research, Research

There are many factors of the restaurant you want to research before making any critical decisions. A great place to start is by looking at the fixed costs of your potential business, the monthly or weekly expense that does not change from invoice period to invoice period. This includes:

- ✓ Rent
- ✓ A mortgage
- ✓ Labour costs
- ✓ Utility costs
- ✓ Permits.

What's the Going Rate for Restaurant Space in your Area:

_____

_____

What's the average cost for cooks, servers, sommeliers and so on?

_____

_____

_____

_____

_____

_____

_____

_____

_____

_____

_____

Beyond fixed costs, it's important to research the local laws associated with opening restaurants.

- ✓ Is there a limit on the number of restaurant permits in your city?
- ✓ Do you have a local legal representative well versed in restaurant and food industry law?

Spend key time on the marketing and branding aspects of your business.

What great names are on your list for your restaurant? (Get ideas from family & friends, too!)

_____

_____

_____
_____
_____
_____
_____
_____
_____
_____
_____
_____
_____
_____
_____
_____

Once you love a name or two, be sure to research if it's been used. Check domain hosts such as *Register* and *GoDaddy* to see if the website name of your restaurant is available, too!

Finally, make sure to research how much time you will need to commit to the business before making any major expenses. If you can only commit five hours a week to your restaurant, it might be best to wait a few years until you can firmly commit more time. An absentee owner tends to accelerate a restaurant's failure, so a firm time commitment to your restaurant is one of the most important elements of financial success.

Building Your Business Plan

When entering the restaurant industry, **your business plan** serves as the roadmap to the operation and future of your business. It provides direction in the day-to-day financials, and allows you to identify many of the important topics mentioned in this workbook. Above all, a well-written business plan is likely to make a larger pool of investors eager to give you money. If you have enough cash to open your dream restaurant, some might say you do not need a business plan. However, self-financed restaurants should always write a business plan, too, in order to judge the success and long term practicality of the business.

A well-written business plan includes:
- ✓ Financials of the restaurant.
- ✓ Marketing and operational details.
- ✓ Branding, including your domain name, a logo, social media pages as well as a creative marketing plan.

Your restaurant business plan conveys this information in a precise, organised, and logical manner, all well-written and grammatically correct.

◆ ◆ ◆ ◆ ◆

EXERCISE: BUSINESS PLAN

Here you will describe the individual topics of your restaurant concept through well-organized bullet points. In the space below are some of the topics you want to include. See what you can begin to describe in this exercise—take notes; do research. **The CONCLUSION Section has space for you to write out All Parts of your Business Plan, transferred from here and other part of ths Workbook. It ALSO has a section to paste or staple colors, pictures, samples and other images. After that is complete, plan on TYPING EVERYTHING UP into a single document, after you complete the workbook**

1. Legal Arrangement of Business:

Describe the legal structure of ownership and responsibility (e.g., LLC, S-Corp, etc.):

_____

_____

_____

_____

_____

_____

2. Restaurant Lease or Purchase

_____

_____

_____

_____

3. Capitalization needs.

This includes the amount of money you expect to need to open the restaurant. (Plan on doubling the amount of money you think you will need to open the restaurant.) In addition to initial capital expenses, also consider *your* expenses for the first twelve months. Calculate the cost of all fixed costs for the first year and add this to your capitalization estimate.Spend a lot of time calculating this value.

_____

_____

_____

_____

_____

_____

_____

_____

_____

_____

_____

_____

_____

_____

_____

_____

_____

_____

_____

_____

_____

_____

_____

_____

_____

4. Business Concept

Present a convincing argument as to why your restaurant idea will be more successful than others with passion, painting a descriptive picture of your goals. Here are some ideas to include:

- o Style of Service (fine dining, quick service, casual, etc.)
- o Ambiance and Décor
- o Seating Capacity
- o Operating Hours
- o Menu Theme
- o Unique Selling Points
- o Related Sales (Catering, Delivery, Retail, etc.)

_____

_____

_____

_____

_____

_____

_____

_____

_____

_____

_____

_____

_____

_____

_____

_____

_____

_____

_____

_____

_____

_____

_____

_____

_____

_____

_____

5. Sample menu

Within the company description, you need to include a sample menu for your restaurant. It helps to attract investors through their stomachs. Ultimately, you want to make sure to add prices and showcase the style of food you plan on selling. (We discuss this in later Units.) Formal restaurants will have lengthy and descriptive menus while fast casual restaurant menus will be short and to the point.

_____

_____

_____

_____

_____

_____

_____

_____

_____
_____
_____
_____
_____
_____
_____
_____
_____
_____
_____
_____
_____
_____
_____
_____
_____
_____
_____
_____
_____
_____
_____
_____
_____
_____
_____
_____
_____

6. Restaurant Design and Layout

Beyond the food and financials, investors will want to gain a great sense of what the space will look like on opening day. To make a convincing and visual argument, try to include architectural drawings of your restaurant concept. Floor plans, kitchen layouts and artistic renderings are all positive elements to add to your business plan. Can you start to sketch out your dream restaurant in the space below?

(As in any Exercise, feel free to use additional paper or start a companion notebook/scrapbook for designs, colors, products, maps— things that contribute to the mood and concept of your dream restaurant!)

MY RESTAURANT LAYOUT

MY RESTAURANT LAYOUT

7. Restaurant Management Team Overview

A successful restaurant is judged not only by competent owners but also by competent management. You will need to select experienced managers in positions of authority. You may not know your managers at this point, but fill it in as you do, or begin your research about your team. Remember: good ownership should not be confused with good management. For this section, collect and include the following elements for your management team overview:

- Management Organizational Chart
- CVs and Biographies of Managers
- Management Contracts for the Restaurant
- Financial Incentives for Managers

_____
_____
_____
_____
_____
_____
_____
_____
_____
_____
_____
_____
_____
_____
_____
_____
_____
_____
_____
_____
_____
_____
_____
_____
_____
_____
_____

_____

_____

_____

_____

8. Restaurant Environment Analysis

Restaurant Environment Analysis is the section of your restaurant business plan that describes the competitive landscape of your market. There are four areas of concentration when writing a restaurant environment analysis:

- o Study Restaurant Trends and Consumer Habits
- o Identify your Target Market
- o Location Analysis
- o Competitive Analysis

You looked at some of these in this Unit's earlier exercise. Flesh those ideas out and include some paragraphs here that could go into section 8 of your Restaurant Business Plan:

_____

_____

_____

_____

_____

_____

_____

_____

_____

_____

_____

_____

_____

_____

_____

_____

_____

_____

_____

_____

_____

_____
_____
_____
_____

9. Restaurant Marketing Strategy

A successful restaurant business plan always includes a well-written marketing plan that paints a picture of your strategy for **before** and **after** the opening. Make sure to distinguish these two marketing goals. Some great ways to build a compelling marketing strategy include:

o Build a Customer Database for Direct Marketing
o Create a Frequent Diner and VIP Programme
o Develop a Compelling Email Campaign
o Promote a Direct Mail Campaign for Your Local Postcode

o Community Involvement such as Charity Events
o Create T-shirts, Hats, Bumper Stickers, Business Cards
o Hire a Public Relations Firm for Media Outreach
o Include an Advertising Budget

Which of these can you describe and include your Restaurant Plan?:

_____
_____
_____
_____
_____
_____
_____
_____
_____
_____
_____
_____
_____
_____
_____
_____
_____
_____

_____

_____

_____

_____

_____

_____

_____

_____

_____

_____

_____

_____

10. Restaurant Operations Plan

The operations plan within your business plan is the largest section of the document. Here, you want to convey the general day-to-day aspects of your operation. While you might not be able to add every detail yet, try to cover the general tasks like a labour schedule for your business and your intended hours of operation. This part also documents the system of controls you will implement in order to hit your financial targets and projections, including:

- Staff Structure
- Employee Training Manual
- Suppliers
- Management Controls
- Point of Sales System
- Expected Labour Schedule
- Time and Attendance Tracking
- Inventory Control Method
- Insurance and Liability Controls
- Administrative Controls
- Cash Controls
- Weekly Profit/Loss Statement
- Method of Bookkeeping
- Payroll Processing

_____

_____

_____

_____

_____

_____

_____

_____

_____

_____

_____

_____

_____

_____

_____

_____

_____

_____

_____

_____

_____

_____

_____

_____

_____

_____

_____

_____

_____

_____

_____

_____

_____

_____

_____

_____

_____

_____

_____

_____

_____

_____

◆ ◆ ◆ ◆ ◆

EXERCISE: EXECUTIVE SUMMARY

Okay, *NOW* you can actually start to think about the very *first part of your business plan*, which is called the **Executive Summary.** It is typically one to four pages in length and introduces your concept to perspective investors. You write the executive summary *after* you have completed the remainder of the plan; that why the exercise is here, after you've done some research, thought, and planning.

A well-written executive summary conveys your restaurant's identity and describes why it will be a successful business venture. In addition to costs, it is important to add the anticipated return on investment early in the summary. Avoid too many specific details, but do add a confidentiality statement before the executive summary starts. **Start your Executive Summary in the space below, then type and transfer it to the beginning of Your Restaurant Business Plan! **WRITE YOUR FULL EXECUTIV SUMMARY IN THE CONCLUSION UNIT AND THE END OF THIS WORKBOOK****

_____
_____
_____
_____
_____
_____
_____
_____
_____
_____
_____
_____
_____
_____
_____
_____
_____
_____
_____
_____
_____
_____
_____
_____
_____
_____
_____
_____
_____
_____

_____

_____

_____

_____

_____

_____

_____

_____

_____

_____

_____

_____

Finding Funding (Investors)

After you finish your **business plan,** it will be time to approach people to gain the necessary financing for your restaurant. Here are some potential places to start:

> - Asking *friends and family*; maybe not the £100,000 investors, but you might find a few people close to you who are willing to stake £5,000
> - *Crowd funding*. Websites such as *Kickstarter* allow people to give money to concepts that benefit a community or bring a new innovation to the world.
> - *Banks* are another source for restaurant financing, although it is becoming more and more difficult to convince them of this risk. If you plan this, what is your collateral? (e.g., your home, cars and other property)
> - *Your personal savings.* To eliminate expenses, open a fully renovated restaurant which requires little initial investment.
> - *Business and credit accounts*

◆◆◆◆

What are your intended sources of income to start your restaurant venture?

_____

_____

_____

_____

_____

♦♦♦♦♦

UNIT 2

CORRECTLY FORMULATING A FOOD SERVICE CONCEPT

To help you develop the concept for *your* new restaurant, this Unit looks at the types and styles or restaurants, levels of formality, alcohol service, architecture, marketing and so on. By learning these basics, you will be able to create a compelling restaurant concept for any style of food service.

The Types and Styles of Restaurants

You will need to identify two major factors when choosing a type and style of restaurant to open. The first factor deals with **the type of restaurant**. Examples include fast food, sit down, formal, and theatric dining, to name a few types of restaurants. The second factor you want to identify relates to the **type of cuisine** you should serve.

From my book, you know the various types of restaurants. Here's a list to recap. In the exercise below, identify which one(s) fit your intended restaurant:

Formal Dining: The most expensive restaurants to eat in and to open, so require major financial investment. Formal dining includes proper linens, sturdy tables, formal service, fancy plates and expensive glassware.

Take-Away /Automat: Where there is very little interaction between the customers and staff. The staff are typically hidden behind a wall.

Bakery: A restaurant that concentrates on the production of breads, desserts, simple sandwiches and salads.

Bar/Pub: A restaurant which mostly sells alcohol and beer. Food is not the focus of most.

Cafeteria: A type of restaurant where the customer chooses foods from large buffet tables; those are placed on a tray and paid for at the end of the buffet line.

Café/Bistro: The most common and popular style of restaurant, a café or bistro is a very comfortable restaurant space and includes a waiter or waitress.

Coffeehouse: A restaurant that focuses on the production and sale of coffee, tea and snacks.

Drive-In: A concept where the customer drives their car onto the restaurant property. The customer orders food from the car window, and a server brings the meal to the car.

Fast Food/Quick Service: Focuses on a low wait time for food. This style of restaurant is a no frills adventure; often is a pre-established franchise.

Food Cart: Perhaps the cheapest type of restaurant to open. Since there is no physical space to decorate and equip, you will find it easy to open a food cart.

Delicatessen: A deli is a type of restaurant that focuses on sandwich and catering sales; popular in business districts.

Diners: Sell a variety of cuisine styles from Italian to Asian. In addition, diners tend to serve their entire menu throughout the day.

Supper club: Typically barely visible to the outside world. Instead, a supper club relies on a good reputation of pleasure seeking foodies

Theme Restaurant: A themed restaurant is a style of food service that includes a fictional element to the ambiance

Then there are all sorts of cuisines by region: **Asian (Chinese, Japanese, Vietnamese, Thai), Indian, Middle Eastern, European, African** in many varieties and nationalities, **American** and its many regions, **South American, Caribbean,** etc. Will you have alcohol and a **bar?**

You also choose between **quick-service, take-away**, and **sit-down.**

◆◆◆◆

THE TYPE & STYLE & CUISINE I ENVISION FOR MY RESTAURANT:

_____
_____
_____
_____
_____
_____
_____
_____
_____
_____
_____
_____

_____

_____

_____

_____

_____

_____

_____

_____

_____

_____

_____

_____

_____

_____

_____

_____

_____

_____

_____

_____

_____

_____

_____

_____

_____

_____

◆ ◆ ◆ ◆

Studying Competition

There are many ways to study competition in the restaurant industry. As we mentioned in Unit 1, you start by looking at the **restaurants closest** to your desired location—anyone else attracting the hungry customer you hope to serve. Study their **types of cuisine** and try to differentiate from these. Study the **cost per person** and make sure to fit within this range. Make sure to pay attention to **slogans, logo and marketing materials** to determine which techniques work best in the local arena.

Beyond your local competition, you should spend some time getting to know your **global competition**. If viable, try to travel to a few cities to get a sense of the menus and flavours of similar restaurant concepts to your own.

Studying competition does not exclusively relate to the physical traits of a restaurant. Today, understanding how your **competition uses social media** is critical for all new restaurants. Follow your competitors on *Facebook* and *Twitter* to comprehend how they reach their customers with daily deals and menu specials.

◆◆◆◆

MY COMPETITORS, LOCALLY & GLOBALLY, AND THEIR FACEBOOK, PINTARIST, TWITTER HANDLES:

_____
_____
_____
_____
_____
_____
_____
_____
_____
_____
_____
_____
_____
_____
_____
_____
_____
_____
_____
_____
_____
_____
_____
_____
_____
_____
_____
_____
_____
_____

_____
_____
_____
_____

◆◆◆◆

Identifying Functions of the Restaurant Space, Fine Dining or Partying

Every restaurant has a unique layout so yours will requires a unique plan. To make this process easy to understand, it is best to **identify functions of your business**. In the exercise below, identify these functions and list them on a piece of paper. As you study the design plans for your restaurant, make sure that each function can be accomplished with the current design plans. Some of these functions include the positioning of the bar, displays, areas for group parties, etc. If not, it might be a good idea to change your plans or find a new restaurant location.

As you map the layout of your restaurant, make sure to account for secondary functions of the business, too. For instance, if you plan on having an extensive _catering business_, it might be a good idea to add additional kitchen and refrigerator space to your business plan and layout designs. If you plan on opening a fine dining restaurant, make sure to leave room for a _linen press_ and a _coat check_ as well as room to _store glassware and wine_. If you plan on serving large parties on a nightly basis, you might decide to choose a restaurant space with _private dining rooms_. You also need to consider the logistics of your operation. For instance, you do not want to be carrying deliveries through the dining room, so make sure to _account for deliveries_ during normal business hours using a different route.

◆◆◆◆

EXERCISE: LIST THE PRIMARY & SECONDARY FUNCTIONS OF YOUR BUSINESS

_____   _____
_____   _____
_____   _____
_____   _____
_____   _____
_____   _____
_____   _____
_____   _____
_____   _____
_____   _____
_____   _____

_____   _____
_____   _____
_____   _____
_____   _____
_____   _____
_____   _____
_____   _____
_____   _____
_____   _____
_____   _____
_____   _____
_____   _____
_____   _____
_____   _____
_____   _____
_____   _____
_____   _____
_____   _____
_____   _____
_____   _____
_____   _____
_____   _____
_____   _____
_____   _____
_____   _____
_____   _____
_____   _____
_____   _____
_____   _____
_____   _____
_____   _____

◆◆◆◆

Marketing and Branding

Marketing your restaurant can be a tricky task to accomplish. Choosing the correct words to describe your restaurant is a lot harder than simply choosing three or four words. Instead, it is important to craft a clear and concise message. Since you only have one shot to reach customers, it is always a good idea to hire a marketing professional before and during your restaurants opening. By hiring a professional, you will find unique ways to reach a large diverse customer base.

It is very important to invest in a convincing marketing and branding campaign. To start, build your brand. You want to focus on creating a compelling name and logo for your business. In the space below, **outline your brand and then begin to craft a short "message" that reflects your vision of your new restaurant.**

◆◆◆

My Brand and My Marketing Message:

_____
_____
_____
_____
_____
_____
_____
_____
_____
_____
_____
_____
_____
_____
_____
_____
_____
_____
_____
_____
_____
_____
_____
_____
_____
_____
_____
_____

◆◆◆◆

UNIT 3

PROPERTY/PREMISES: TO BUY OR TO LEASE?

Choosing the correct location for your restaurant is immensely important. While the High Street might seem like the best way to reach customers, some restaurants have become successful by being off the beaten path. It's important to find the balance between what a property costs and the amount of traffic the location receives. When opening a restaurant, a confusing part of the process is deciding this about your property: to rent or lease. In this Unit, we will look at how to make the best decision for your restaurant concept.

Location, Location, Location

The location of your restaurant is a very, very, very important aspect of your business. For quick service restaurants, the busier the area the better. You need a high degree of foot traffic to increase sales. On the other hand, some restaurants do very well when they are not located in busy areas of town. This is particularly true for destination venues where customers come in groups and therefore are likely to be driving, which requires parking spaces. As another example, a town or village known for its rest and relaxation can be a great place to open a restaurant, provided it gets the proper amount of weekend traffic.

Then, as you look at various sites, you consider the **buying** or **leasing** question from this point of view. Buying a restaurant is a *major financial decision* which a *long term commitment*. If you have limited funds to open your restaurant, you are very unlikely to buy a property. People who buy a restaurant and property have typically been in the restaurant business for a while or have significant capital.

The most important factor, along with having a first rate restaurant, is a location's *ability to attract customers*. An attractive property in a well-travelled area can be a smart investment. However, you need to be meticulous when doing your research. Considering the purchase as a long-term commitment: does your dream location have a history of economic stability?

Most restaurant owners **begin their empire by leasing.** This financial arrangement allows new restaurant owners to free up capital for marketing, equipment, and architectural additions to their property. As a restaurant grows in popularity, many owners decide to allow their lease to expire and open a restaurant on their own property. While this is a great long-term goal, the reality is you will most likely start as a renter.

Before you sign a restaurant lease, it is important to understand what the landlord will and will not allow you to modify. The space needs to have the wiring, ventilation, and plumbing to house a restaurant, and with that in mind, you may or may not need to do some remodelling to bring the facility up to your standards as well as up to code. Be sure to clearly understand which expenses you will be responsible for and what expenses the owner will be responsible for.

EXERCISE: LOCATION

To start sketching your ideas for an ideal restaurant location, first determine how many customers you will need on a weekly or daily basis. Now compare this data to the traffic you expect for the area you are considering. Outline these in your notes below.

Considering ideas and areas you have for your new restaurant, also include your thoughts about purchase v. rent. Buying may not even be a financial option; then just focus on the considerations *you* need for potential leases. If you have the capital and real estate opportunity, do a comparison in the space below between buying and renting a space for your restaurant:

_____
_____
_____
_____
_____
_____
_____
_____
_____
_____
_____
_____
_____
_____
_____
_____
_____
_____
_____

◆ ◆ ◆ ◆ ◆

Parking, entrance, frontage, inside set up, kitchen, bar location, facilities & Creative Arrangements

For one last aspect of your Location exercise, look back at the specific needs of your business model, and in the space below sketch out details that you want to include on your "location shopping list" or that you can check out at your selected location.

For instance, if you plan on opening a restaurant in the country, do you have a car park large enough to accommodate your maximum number of clients? If your restaurant plans on receiving a lot of walk-in business, what is compelling and comforting about your restaurant frontage? It is also important to consider the needs of the kitchen. Will the cooks have enough room to prep and cook the meals? Do you have enough room to add lockers for the employees? Will there be enough room for dry storage? These are just a few questions you need to ask yourself when planning the layout of your space.

In some cases, the prestige of bringing a well-known restaurant into a prime location can land you a very favorable leasing arrangement and financing. For this reason, if you have enjoyed some amount of fame in the food or celebrity world, make sure to *emphasize this fame* when it's time to negotiate the lease or business plan. Both landlords and banks are open to these sorts of arrangements, so try to be creative if needed.

◆◆◆◆

Additional Aspects for Consideration or Research at My Dream Restaurant Location

_____
_____
_____
_____
_____
_____
_____
_____
_____
_____
_____
_____
_____
_____
_____

◆◆◆◆◆

UNIT 4

THE BASICS OF RUNNING A RESTAURANT

nce you go through the process of writing a business plan and finding investors, it will be time to start building the basics you need to run your restaurant. You will want to note that, as you fulfill your pre-opening tasks, your strategies will change. You should plan to update your business plan from time to time, including your projected profit margin when you finally contact your suppliers and get up-to-date price quotes. Update the financial information when you find your restaurant property, too. Your business plan will be a *dynamic guide to opening your restaurant*.

Also plan to *update your investors* from time to time with your progress opening the restaurant. Make sure to inform them of major changes to your financial outlook, especially if you accomplish a task for less money than needed! Tell them how you plan on using those extra funds within the project. Having an open and transparent relationship with your investors will prove beneficial in the long term.

Setting up the operations

To start your restaurant, you will need to **outline the process you will use to open the restaurant.** Setting up your operations can be a complex task to manage. There are many major functions you need to accomplish months ahead of the opening. If you miss these dates, you might delay the opening for months, which means months of rent and payments. **Make sure to take great care when setting up your operations.**

Beyond the logistics of the opening, make sure to *consider the season of your opening*. In some regions, your target audience might only be around for three to six months. If you open a restaurant in a holiday town out of season, for example, your restaurant will remain dormant until the next season starts.

In this next Exercise, you will clearly write your operational objectives into a well-organized list. Make sure to add each element that is important to your unique restaurant. A few objectives that you might need to add to your list include:

- ✓ Obtain Liquor or Alcohol Permits
- ✓ Set up Food Suppliers
- ✓ Order Glasses, Plates and Silverware
- ✓ Order Menus

- ✓ Test Recipes
- ✓ Set up Wine Accounts
- ✓ Set up Beverage Accounts
- ✓ Set up Sanitation Accounts
- ✓ Restaurant Kitchen Tasks
- ✓ Restaurant Bar Tasks

This list of topics will continue to grow and your understanding will deepen as you read this workbook and develop a greater sense of what's important to your particular restaurant.

◆◆◆◆

My List of Steps & Priorities for Opening My Dream Restaurant

_____
_____
_____
_____
_____
_____
_____
_____
_____
_____
_____
_____
_____
_____
_____
_____
_____
_____
_____
_____
_____
_____
_____
_____
_____

_____
_____
_____
_____
_____
_____
_____
_____
_____
_____
_____
_____
_____
_____
_____
_____
_____
_____
_____
_____
_____
_____
_____
_____

Plan to come back to this exercise and this list as you explore more of this workbook. Also plan to develop **a timeline to Opening** which will draw from this list and put each step on a Calendar.

◆◆◆◆

Dealing with suppliers and procurement

Each restaurant has their own unique set of suppliers. To make sure you hire the correct number of suppliers, as well as finding a supplier for EVERY 'ingredient' of the restaurant, carefully track your supply and ingredient inventory lists during the pre-opening.. This is one of the most important tasks you need to accomplish during the pre-opening: the supply of the many foods and goods to your restaurant. By remaining organized when finding suppliers, you will find the opening of your restaurant a much more peaceful process

At minimum, you are likely to have **three or four food suppliers.** Most wholesale suppliers specialize in one category of food. So, depending on your type of establishment, you may need:

- ✓ A Meat Supplier
- ✓ Fish Supplier
- ✓ Vegetable Supplier
- ✓ Dry Goods Supplier
- ✓ Wine and liquor suppliers
- ✓ Supplier for paper goods & specialty packaging companies, especially if for a fast food or quick service restaurant
- ✓ Office supplies, like from Staples
- ✓ A linen supply company to launder or rent napkins and tablecloths
- ✓ Beverage supplier (e.g., Coke or Pepsi and other soft drinks in bulk)

Some restaurants use very large companies which service all these goods, but large companies are difficult to negotiate with and tend to sell perishable goods not on par with their specialist counterparts. Do some research to complete the exercise below. Also research if your potential Dry Goods supplier has, beyond ketchup, flour and sugar, also cleaning supplies and kitchen supplies, for example, so you can order detergent for your dishwasher, pot scrubbers, aluminium foil and paper products at the same time.

◆◆◆◆

EXERCISE: Food Supplies I Will Need and Potential Suppliers

SUPPLIES I NEED	SUPPLIERS
_____	_____
_____	_____
_____	_____
_____	_____
_____	_____
_____	_____
_____	_____
_____	_____
_____	_____
_____	_____
_____	_____
_____	_____

_____   _____
_____   _____
_____   _____
_____   _____
_____   _____
_____   _____
_____   _____
_____   _____
_____   _____
_____   _____
_____   _____
_____   _____
_____   _____
_____   _____
_____   _____
_____   _____

◆ ◆ ◆ ◆ ◆

Make sure to **contact suppliers at least six weeks before you plan on opening;** and to make sure you have enough time to taste, it is a good idea to contact your **wine company at least two months before** the opening. Some local governments require that your liquor licence be approved before receiving alcohol from suppliers, so take care of this task early in the operations process. It is always a good idea to **interview more than one supplier**, so make sure to invite a number of companies to discuss your needs and their abilities. Discuss:

> ➤ The line of products they sell
> ➤ The minimum orders
> ➤ Their delivery days
> ➤ Credit terms
> ➤ Your opening date and contracts.

Also discover if some items, like select grades of products or specific spicing or specialty items, **are not deliverable**. These, you must plan to buy directly.

◆ ◆ ◆ ◆ ◆

Management and Production

In order to maintain a steady and quality production, management needs to be present at all times. For instance, you need to make sure a Sous Chef is always present in the kitchen to deal with any unexpected events. It is important to have the bar manager present for at least five days of the week, and the same can be said for the Maître D.

It is also extremely important to keep careful track of your finances. To accomplish this goal without serious problems down the road, make sure to ***save every receipt to receive and process***. If you retain every invoice and receipt, both incoming and outgoing, you can manage your finances no matter what happens. While technology helps to manage the finances of a restaurant, technology also breaks down from time to time.

Plan on analyzing your financial data on a week-to-week basis. In order to correctly determine the profit or loss for the week, you will need to know the **Gross Receipts** for the week as well as **the cost of goods**. By having this information handy and well organized, it becomes easier to put together an accurate picture of your financial state

Money matters: Identifying Fixed Costs and Variable Costs

You do not want too many employees being able to handle the money, or you can expect a fair amount of theft. Instead, hold the ***managers responsible for handling cash.*** Beyond accepting cash from your guests, you might need to make payments to suppliers via cash. In this case, a petty cash drawer is needed. Install a safe so that you can take care of the nightly keep at your bank on the following business day.

As soon as possible, it is important to get an early sense of ***your fixed costs*** and ***variable costs.*** Fixed costs are costs you will incur every month, no matter how busy your restaurant is. Variable costs depend on how busy you are on a month-to-month basis. An example of a fixed cost includes your rent; and a variable cost is the cost of ingredients.

In the Exercise below, begin to rough in a budget for each. For fixed costs, you need to consider:

- ✓ Rent
- ✓ Water
- ✓ Electric
- ✓ Gas
- ✓ Permits

✓ All full-time employees' wages.

Variable costs are set by how busy you are, both for your food and your labor. These are complicated but begin to imagine your own restaurant, when it will tend to be busy, what things you can plan for or ways to reduce expense.

◆◆◆◆◆

EXERCISE:

List Some of your Anticipated FIXED & VARIABLE Costs Below; Include rough Amounts!

FIXED COSTS + $/Week	VARIABLE COSTS + $/Week
_____	_____
_____	_____
_____	_____
_____	_____
_____	_____
_____	_____
_____	_____
_____	_____
_____	_____
_____	_____
_____	_____
_____	_____
_____	_____
_____	_____
_____	_____
_____	_____
_____	_____
_____	_____
_____	_____

_____   _____
_____   _____
_____   _____
_____   _____
_____   _____
_____   _____
_____   _____

◆◆◆◆◆

Food Safety

In my book, *A Recipe for Restaurant Success,* I outline many guidelines for how to prepare and serve foods in a safe manner. Millions of people become sick each year and thousands die after eating contaminated or mishandled foods. Serving safe food has numerous benefits. By preventing food-borne illness outbreaks, establishments can avoid legal fees, medical claims, wasted food, bad publicity and possibly, closure of the restaurant.

Your responsibility as Restaurateur is to develop your own checklist and set of policies for food handling (receiving, storage, cooling, cross-contamination, preparation, re-heating, touched surfaces, etc.) and for your food-service workers (cleanliness, uniforms, jewelry and hair rules, etc.) In the space below, outline your top principles for food safety in cleanliness, uniforms, jewelry and hair rules, hand-washing, etc.). In the space below, outline:

MY TOP PRINCIPLES FOR FOOD SAFETY in My Dream Restaurant:

_____
_____
_____
_____
_____
_____
_____
_____
_____
_____

♦♦♦♦♦

How to Create Schedules, Rotas

Depending on the type of restaurant you decide to open (e.g., quick-serve v. fine dining) and where (countries have different rules and habits), your staff schedules will vary greatly.

Unlike many other business models, scheduling for the restaurant is key to portraying the message of being organized, efficient and reliable; all of which are primary considerations for a diner. make sure to ask the staff what their preferred method of scheduling is.

1. Determine the hours of your restaurant. (e.g., If you open for breakfast, lunch and dinner, you will need a much larger staff compared to a 'dinner only' restaurant)

2. Decide how many staff you need for each hour of the week. Create a diagram with seven columns, each representing a day of the week. Next, add rows to represent each position you need to fill. Determine how many hours you will need the employee to work, then use this number as a shift. (Just front of house hours.) Have the maximum amount of employees during dinner and lunch hours.

3. For the kitchen schedule, most restaurants have two crews; one working during the day and one working at night. The day crew gets to work before the restaurant opens to receive foods and prep. As lunch beings, the dinner crew arrives, and both crews serve lunch and prep for dinner. As dinner arrives, the day crew leaves. When it is time to create your kitchen schedule, ask your chef to draw the above-mentioned diagram and determine how many cooks will be needed and for which hours

4. try and offer your administrative staff normal working hours, Monday to Friday, 9am to 5pm. There is no need to hire an accountant during the weekend, so keep this crew well organised during the day.

Below are two **sample kitchen schedules.** Then do the **Exercise** to figure your front-of-house schedule.

JOB POSITION	MON HRS	Cost ($)	HRS (#)	TUES HRS	Cost ($)	HRS (#)	WED HRS	Cost ($)	HRS (#)	THURS HRS	Cost ($)	HRS (#)	FRI HRS	Cost ($)	HRS (#)	SAT HRS	Cost ($)	HRS (#)	SUN HRS	Cost ($)	HRS (#)
Server	9 - 5	17	8	9 - 5	17	8	9 - 5	17	8	9 - 5	17	8	9 - 5	17	8	9 - 5	17	8	9 - 5	17	8
Server	10 - 3	11	5	10 - 3	11	5	9 - 2	11	5	9 - 2	11	5	9 - 2	11	5	9 - 2	11	5	10 - 3	11	5
Server	10 - 3	11	5	10 - 3	11	5	10 - 3	11	5	10 - 3	11	5	10 - 3	11	5	10 - 3	11	5	10 - 3	11	5
Server	10 - 3	11	5	10 - 3	11	5	10 - 3	11	5	10 - 3	11	5	10 - 3	11	5	10 - 3	11	5	10 - 3	11	5
Server	11 - 8	19	9	11 - 8	19	9	10 - 3	11	5	10 - 3	11	5	10 - 3	11	5	10 - 3	11	5	11 - 8	19	9
Server				3 - 9	13	6	11 - 8	19	9	11 - 8	13	9	11 - 8	19	9	11 - 8	19	9	3 - 9	13	6
Server	4 - 10	13	6	4 - 10	13	6	3 - 9	13	6	3 - 9	13	6	3 - 9	13	6	3 - 9	13	6	4 - 10	13	6
Server	6 - 11	11	5	6 - 11	11	5	4 - 10	11	6	4 - 10	11	6	4 - 10	11	6	4 - 10	11	6	6 - 11	11	5
Server							6 - 11	11	5	6 - 11	11	5	4 - 11	15	7	4 - 11	15	7			
Server													6 - 11	11	5	6 - 11	11	5			
Grill	8 - 4	72	8	8 - 4	72	8	8 - 4	72	8	8 - 4	72	8	8 - 4	72	8	8 - 4	72	8	8 - 4	72	8
Fry	9 - 3	54	6	9 - 3	54	6	9 - 3	54	6	9 - 3	54	6	9 - 3	54	6	9 - 3	54	6	9 - 3	54	6
Grill	4 - 11	63	7	4 - 11	63	7	4 - 11	63	7	4 - 11	63	7	4 - 11	63	7	4 - 11	63	7	4 - 11	63	7
Fry	5 - 11	54	6	5 - 11	54	6	5 - 11	54	6	5 - 11	54	6	5 - 11	54	6	5 - 11	54	6	5 - 11	54	6
Dishes	8 - 4	48	8	8 - 4	48	8	8 - 4	48	8	8 - 4	48	8	8 - 4	48	8	8 - 4	48	8	8 - 4	48	8
Dishes	5 - 11	36	6	5 - 11	36	6	5 - 11	36	6	5 - 11	36	6	5 - 11	36	6	5 - 11	36	6	5 - 11	36	6
TOTALS:	MON	419	84	TUES	431	90	WED	442	95	THUR	457	95	FRI	457	102	SAT	457	102	SUN	431	90

Weekly Total: $3,079
Hours: 659

KITCHEN SCHEDULE

DATE	7/12/2009 SUNDAY	7/13/2009 MONDAY	7/14/2009 TUESDAY	7/15/2009 WEDNESDAY	7/16/2009 THURSDAY	7/17/2009 FRIDAY	7/18/2009 SATURDAY
CHEF		ON	ON	ON	ON	ON	
SOUS CHEF	10 A - 6:30	10:30 A - 6:30 A	10:30 A - 6:30 P	10 A - 6:30 P	10:30 A - 6:30 P		
BAKER			7:30 A - 2 P	7:30 A - 2 P	7:30 A - 2 P	6:30 A - 4 P	6:30 A - 2 P
AM COOK	6:30 A - 11 A	6:30 A - 2 P	6:30 A - 2 P	6:30 A - 2 P	6:30 A - 2 P		
PM COOK	9:30 A - 6:30 P	9:30 A - 6:30 P			9:30 A - 6:30 P	9:30 A - 6:30 P	9 A - 6:30 P
PM COOK	7:30 A - 11 A	7:30 A - 11 A	10 A - 2 P			9:30 A - 6:30 P	9 A - 6:30 P
PREP COOK			3 P - 6:30 P	9:30 A - 6:30 P	10 A - 2 P	10 A - 5 P	7:30 A - 11 A
DISHWASHER	8 A - 2:30 P	8 A - 2:30 P	8 A - 2:30 P			7:30 A - 2:30 P	8 A - 2:30 P
DISHWASHER	5 P - 8 P			8 A - 2:30 P	8 A - 2:30 P		5 P - 8 P
DISHWASHER		5 P - 8 P	5 P - 8 P	5 P - 8 P	5 P - 8 P	5 P - 8 P	
DISHWASHER		5 P - 8 P	5 P - 8 P	5 P - 8 P	5 P - 8 P	5 P - 8 P	

ANY SHIFT 6 HOURS OR MORE REQUIRES 1/2 HOUR BREAK!

PLEASE CLOCK IN AND OUT ON THE CORRECT TIMES
ACCORDING TO YOUR SCHEDULE!

SCHEDULE SUBJECT TO CHANGE AT ANY TIME WITHOUT NOTICE!

MY DRAFT FRONT-OF-HOUSE SCHEDULE

POST	MON	TUES	WED	THURS	FRI	SAT	SUN

◆ ◆ ◆ ◆ ◆

UNIT 5

BUILDING THE BEST STAFF

he structure of your restaurant staff will vary depending on the type and style of restaurant you open. However, most sit-down restaurants tend to follow a standard staff structure. For this reason, my book and workbook discusses the positions found in a normal, sit-down restaurant.

The Key Positions of Restaurant Staff

Beyond the owners, the most important person in a restaurant, and the person with the most responsibility, is the **General Manager**. You want to hire someone with lots of experience plus a high degree of patience and hospitality. The general manager runs the day-to-day aspects of the business, interacts with customers, solicits the media, to name a few tasks. When hiring your initial staff, you want to first hire the general manager.

Beyond the general manager, other staff positions can be divided into two groups: **Front of House** and **Back of House**. Overall, always try to hire staff who have a very similar demeanour to the general manager. And make sure to call and check references to assure yourself as customer service, quality, and hospitality will then priorities of everyone on your team

Front of House

The highest position in the Front of House is typically the **Maître d'Hotel**. In many restaurants, the Maitre D. and the General Manager are the same person; it is only in very large formal restaurants where these two positions are divided into individual staff. The Maitre D. is responsible for *making sure the guests are happy* with the dining experience, takes care of the VIPs as well as ensure that the front of house staff are performing their tasks with a high degree of integrity and formality.

The next highest position is the **Director of Beverages,** who is responsible for managing the bar and wine programs; they deal with supplier relations directly related to the drinks served at your restaurant. This might include wine companies, beer companies, soda suppliers, and bar supply companies.

Most restaurants have a **Sommelier** and a **Mixologist** under the Director of Beverages. A sommelier *runs and directs the wine program* of the restaurant. The Mixologist is the person who *runs the bar program.*

Beyond beverages, the Front of House staff will include a number of people to assist with service. The *service is typically run* by **Captain**s, a group of waiters who are responsible for taking orders, describing the menu, interacting with the guests, among other tasks. Once the food is prepared in the kitchen, another member of the staff, the **Runner**, will *bring the food to the table.* Restaurants often have **Servers,** who purpose is to *remove plates from the table, replace napkins, refill water glasses, and other tasks, such as clearing the tables in between courses.*

Back of House

In terms of Back of House positions, the *kitchen is run* by the **Executive Chef.** Directly underneath the Executive Chef is the **Pastry Chef** and **Chef de Cuisine.** While the Executive Chef is responsible to running the entire kitchen, the Pastry Chef is responsible for *running the pastry section* of the kitchen. The Chef de Cuisine *runs the remainder of the kitchen* on a day-to-day basis. Below the Chef de Cuisine, most restaurants will have **Sous Chefs**. A Sous Chef *manages the moment-to-moment tasks of the kitchen and assures the correct inventory has been ordered* for each day of service.

Beneath the Sous Chefs, each station of the kitchen is run by cooks known as **Chef de Parties**. This position is *responsible for managing each station of the kitchen:* the Cold Food, Fish Station, Meat Station, and Vegetable Station. Below the Chef de Partie, the **cooks** of the restaurant are responsible for *preparing the food for their particular station.* Many kitchens also include cooks whose sole purpose is to *prepare vegetables, meat or fish.* Depending on the size of your operation, you may or may not need **prep cooks**. Finally, the last position in the kitchen, and certainly one of the most important positions in the restaurant, are the **Kitchen Assistants**, who *load the dishwashers.*

Building a Better Front of House & Kitchen Staff

➤ Try to hold regular meetings with the staff to address concerns, complexities and stories of interest.
➤ Share your thoughts with the staff, as well as learn from their input; this will benefit your service greatly.
➤ Offer short courses to the staff, such as wine tastings and cheese education courses through local experts. It's a fantastic way to increase the knowledge of your restaurant staff.
➤ Offer financial bonuses based on performance

The most important and challenging aspect of your kitchen relates to quality. It is very important to serve the same quality of food every time a dish leaves the kitchen.

> ➢ Remember your *chef is the person who is responsible for the quality of the food*. With this said, you need to make sure you give your chef the proper tools to maintain a high quality
> ➢ Build in your kitchen *the universal cook*. It's important to teach each member of the staff how to prepare each dish on the menu. That way, if a kitchen worker does not show for work or is sick, the quality of the food will not suffer

◆◆◆◆◆

How to Hire Staff

One of the hardest tasks to successfully navigate when opening a restaurant involves the hiring of staff. There are many places to search for employees, so it is important to invest your time and energy in the correct direction. Luckily, there are many online sources for finding employees. Beyond online, many regions and countries have employment agencies which offer a wide variety of staff potentials. Before deciding which direction you would like to go, create a budget in terms of advertising expenses and time.

In many countries, websites such as *Craigslist* are a great way to find employees. While there is typically a small cost to place ads, you are sure to receive many potential candidates from this sort of website. When hiring your initial crew of managers, make sure to place a different advertisement for each position. Once you have hired your initial staff, it is a good idea to ask them if they know of people who might be good employees fit for the new restaurant. Most managers prefer to bring an employee or two from their previous place of employment.

When hiring, each position should have a different interview focus Make sure to **involve the general manager during the front of house interviews**. In fact, it is best to let the general manager organize the process. The **same strategy works well for the chef.** With years of experience, the chef will be able to determine which potential employees will work best for the concept and tone of the kitchen. It is important to review the CVs of each potential candidate with the general manager and chef to determine if a candidate is fit for the position, is being offered the correct salary, potential worries, etc.

The final aspect relating to hiring involves **the 'When' part of the equation**. You definitely want to hire the key managers of the restaurant well before the opening. However, you do not have to hire every member of the crew months before the opening.

◆◆◆◆◆

EXERCISE: YOUR HIRING PLAN

In this exercise, begin to sketch out *who* you will hire for your restaurant, *what their names are* if you happen to have a GM or chef already in place, *what staff* you will need for Front of House, *what staff* for Back of House and how many. Identify any strategies you already have in mind for staffing select positions.

My GM & CHEF:

_____

_____

_____

_____

_____

_____

_____

_____

_____

_____

_____

_____

_____

_____

_____

_____

_____

_____

_____

_____

_____

_____

◆◆◆◆◆

MY FRONT OF HOUSE TEAM:

_____
_____
_____
_____
_____
_____

◆◆◆◆◆

MY BACK OF HOUSE TEAM:

_____
_____
_____
_____
_____
_____
_____
_____
_____
_____
_____
_____
_____
_____
_____
_____
_____
_____
_____
_____
_____
_____
_____
_____
_____

_____
_____
_____
_____
_____
_____
_____
_____
_____
_____
_____
_____
_____
_____

◆◆◆◆◆

Employee Induction and Training

The best way to share the general rules of the restaurant is to construct an **employee manual.** This way, you are guaranteed to train all employees in the exact same way. Employees get a written copy of the rules, making it easy for them to follow the rules and refer to the book when needed. With this said, not all employees should be given the same employee manual.

When you start up your restaurant, there will be many new people and lots of activity right up front. Here are two things I recommend you add to your **pre-opening calendar:**

➤ Set up a general meeting with all employees before the doors open. Ask each employee to introduce themselves to their co-workers.

➤ Beyond the introduction, try and have an informal tasting during the introduction. This allows each employee to taste each dish before discussing with the customers, and provides a valuable introduction to your concept.

The best time to have this introduction party is three days or so before the opening.

As regards training the employees, as you know by now, the general manager and chef are responsible for the overall training of the staff. But this is your restaurant, and you will establish all of the rules—from theme, ambiance, focus, customer strategy, dress and presentation, food and employee safety—everything!

Not only will **an employee manual** make the process easy for you in terms of time, you are guaranteed to train all employees in the exact same way. To make sure the manual is simple to understand and direct, it is best to *create versions for the front of house and back of house*. The overall manual may be elaborate but it must remain operational. A manual should be available for employees to view and review, but it is not practical to give a manual to *every* employee. Instead, **summaries that will be at the fingertips of your employees for quick reference**, especially in key areas that deal with the everyday operations, are the best way to drive home ways of working.

When creating the front of house and back of house manuals, **both copies should have the exact same introduction**. For instance, the *human resource contact* for your restaurant will be the same for the front and back of house, so you might as well make this contact section the exact same. *Pay day* will be the same, and the *local requirements for informing employees* will be the same. Beyond the formalities of employment, make sure to discuss the *philosophy of the restaurant, how to file complaints*, as well as *incentives for great performance*. With this said, it is important to discuss *reasons for terminating employment* as well as the *disciplinary actions* which might take place should a serious infraction occur.

When constructing the **back of house manual**, it is a good idea to *introduce the chef as well as the style of the restaurant*. Spend time discussing *protocols for vacation days, sick days, clocking in, and so on*. When constructing the **front of house manual,** the *more general information you put in the manual, the better*. For instance, you will want to discuss in detail the *instructions for using the Point of Sales system*. Make sure to discuss *the rules of service*: how to serve guests, the proper way to set the tables, etc., before discussing service tasks and after-service tasks. As you move beyond the opening, the rules of your operation might change from time to time. For this reason, it's a good idea to *update your Employee Manuals from time to time*.

◆◆◆◆◆

EXERCISE: YOUR EMPLOYEE MANUAL

This is a big project, and you will just start to **outline your Employee Manual** here in this workbook. But many of these ideas apply to you, so note them down here in as much detail as comes to mind. It is also great to *borrow another successful Employee Manual* as a template, and to remind you of all the topics you need to cover.

My Employee Manual Will Include:

_____
_____
_____
_____
_____
_____
_____
_____
_____
_____
_____
_____
_____
_____
_____
_____
_____
_____
_____
_____
_____
_____
_____
_____
_____
_____
_____
_____
_____
_____
_____
_____
_____
_____
_____
_____
_____
_____
_____
_____
_____
_____
_____
_____

UNIT 6

COMPOSING THE MENU AND FOOD SERVICE DELIVERY

orming an enticing menu is not just the key to pleasing your audience. It is also the key in terms of profit. You need to study your costs and profit margins and emphasize items that maximize your profit margin.

Every type of restaurant requires a unique menu presentation. Formal French restaurants are divided into sections such as Fish, Meat, Soups, Salads and Starters. A quick service restaurant will have a much shorter menu and menu descriptions, and often include photos. For this workbook, we are going to begin our discussion of menu science with the **casual, modern restaurant**. It tends to draw from both formal and quick service concepts.

There are some tricks to menu success for this type of restaurant. For instance, items menu with the best profit margin tend to be isolated in boxes on the menu under a section entitled *House Specials*. You can often add to the meal total of a table if you *make the starters section menu larger* than the main course section, to draw eyes to the appetizers. Try *adding beverages* within this menu design as well, especially beer and mixed drinks, which have a high profit margin.

Remember: the goal is to create a menu that is attractive to the consumer and helps to facilitate a greater profit margin. In order to maximize this relationship, you might consider hiring a professional to design your menu. Having a specialist take a look at your menu will pay for itself within weeks of opening. However, to give you a greater sense of your menu design, the following chapter discusses the basics of great menu science.

The Basics of Menu Science

Starters and Bites

Selling starters is *one of the best ways to add to the price of each meal* at your restaurant. In fact, if you can get your customer to order a starter, you can typically increase the price per guest by 25% to 50%. Create a diverse set of starters. Make sure to include a few salads on the menu, especially since most consumers are looking for healthy dining options. Soups are a great addition to any menu, as are vegetarian dishes. Add a variety of fish and meat dishes. Serving a raw fish plate or sushi makes an attractive addition to many menus, but remember, you need to make sure the fish your serve on the raw plate is of very high quality and freshness. If you cannot guarantee these conditions, it's best to leave the raw fish off the menu.

A controversial component of starter items includes the *selling of small portions of main course dishes*. You want your customers to order an appetizer and main course, not two appetizers. To avoid this, it is best to keep the starters and main courses separate. However, there are a few cases in which main courses can be served as starters. Many starter menus contain a party platter that can be shared with the whole table. In this case, adding samples of a dinner menu can be a great idea.

◆◆◆◆◆

MY RESTAURANT STARTERS IDEAS

_____

_____

_____

_____

_____

_____

_____

_____

_____

_____

_____

_____

_____

_____

_____

_____

_____

_____

_____

_____

_____

_____

_____

_____

◆ ◆ ◆ ◆ ◆

The Main Menu

The way you set up your restaurant menu is highly dependent on the type of restaurant you open. If you open a fine dining restaurant, it is important to offer a set or a la carte menu. If you open a tapas or ethnic restaurant, you might want to create a menu which allows the customers to choose from a number of options and combinations. Make sure to study concepts which are similar to yours in order to find the correct balance when it comes to creating your main menu.

When composing the main menu of your restaurant, there are a number of options to consider. Many restaurants like to serve a menu which is set and does not vary. Other restaurants prefer a format which allows the guests to pick and choose from the main menu as desired. The type and style of your restaurant will determine which main menu format works best for you.

For formal restaurants, the main menu can be either *a la carte* or set. A set menu in a formal restaurant is typically a three, five or seven course endeavour and does not allow for many substitutions. Beware, this type of menu can be tricky to serve.

Some restaurants serve a menu which allows the customer to choose a great variety of tastes. This is especially true in ethnic and tapas restaurants. For instance, the customer might order a standard protein and choose from a variety of vegetable and starch options. If this is the case, you need to make sure you offer a wide variety of options. Sometimes it pays to offer your sides with a set price for a number of sides. For instance, offer three sides for £5. Make sure to place the most profitable options at the top of the menu.

◆◆◆◆◆

MY RESTAURANT MAIN MENU IDEAS

◆ ◆ ◆ ◆ ◆

Desserts

The dessert menu is one of the most important additions to your restaurant. By convincing your guests to purchase a dessert, you increase the cost per person, which certainly helps the bottom line. Besides ordering a delectable dessert, the guest will most likely order a coffee or an after-dinner drink. While you can expect a normal profit margin with the dessert, you can expect a high profit margin for the coffee and liqueur. A great combination.

Besides desserts, the dessert menu should include a selection of coffees, teas and after dinner cocktails. It is a good idea to include a few creative coffees as well, since this sort of after-dinner drink is highly prized by younger restaurant guests. In terms of alcoholic drinks, it is always a good idea to keep digestifs, such as Cognac and Calvados, on the menu. Creating a warm cocktail as an after-dinner drink tends to be an attractive addition to the menu as well, so make sure to remain creative with your dessert cocktails.

To serve a high variety of desserts while maintaining a profit, offer three desserts for a set price. This type of service will make your dessert course stand out from the competition. Another great way to build a popular dessert menu includes creating "off the menu: items. Many pastry chefs are always experimenting and working towards the next great dessert. Ask your pastry chef to keep a few recipes close for these special creations. This tends to keep the pastry chef happy and brings an element of surprise to the meal.

◆◆◆◆◆

MY RESTAURANT DESSERTS IDEAS

_____
_____
_____
_____
_____
_____
_____
_____
_____
_____
_____
_____
_____
_____
_____
_____

◆ ◆ ◆ ◆ ◆

Bar and Beverage

It is a good idea to create a compelling bar service. In order to share your creative drinks with the customers, you need to describe each drink well. For instance, if you create twelve cocktails for your menu, you also need to create twelve in-depth descriptors for the menu. Using highly descriptive and compelling words can help to sell a drink .

Most restaurants have a large and comfortable bar to allow newly arrived guests to relax and wait for their table. For this reason, customers tend to spend a lot of time looking in the direction of the bar, so it's important to highlight your bar program, if possible. For instance, fill the wall behind the bar with *your cocktail specials and descriptors*. Place your beverage menu in this sort of open space.

At the same time, it is important to write a *comprehensive bar menu*. Here, you want to list your specialty cocktails, wine selections, beer selections, types of liquors, sodas, teas and coffee. Sometimes, the restaurant might run out of a certain type of wine or add a wine to the menu. As you can imagine, you do not want to print a new menu every time you decided to add or remove a wine. For this reason, you might *consider serving a daily wine menu* which lists the specials and deletions.

Pricing is important for correct profit margin in both food and beverages. Your restaurant can end up making half its money from the kitchen and half from the bar. The profit margin for the booze is greater, however it is the kitchen, typically, that draws a crowd. So the relationship of the bar to kitchen is very important. To price your foods, the first place to turn should be *your competition*. Make sure to study their menus to determine what prices they charge for each item. Also pay attention to the *portion size*. Once you have this data, it is time study your own menu data.

Determine the cost for each recipe. Study your invoices and portion sizes to determine an educated guess in terms of the overall recipe cost; it should be around 25% of the price of a dish, so simply multiply the cost by 4. For example, if it costs you £5 to create a dish, you should charge £20 for the dish. This makes sure you account for the cost of labour, gas, equipment, and so on.

Next, *compare this data to your competitors*. If your costs and prices are higher, you might want to reduce the price of your dish or cut the size of the portion. In most restaurants, a few dishes will be offered which give the restaurant a smaller profit margin.

As a standard profit margin, most restaurants charge *400% over the cost of the beverage*. For instance, if the cost of a bottle of beer to you is £2, you should charge £8. The same profit margin for wine should be expected, while cocktails can create very high profit margins for the restaurant. With a carefully constructed cocktail, you can see a return of up to 1000%.

♦♦♦♦♦

MY RESTAURANT BARS & BEVERAGE IDEAS

_____
_____
_____
_____
_____
_____
_____
_____
_____
_____
_____
_____
_____
_____
_____
_____
_____
_____
_____
_____
_____
_____
_____
_____
_____
_____
_____
_____
_____
_____
_____
_____
_____
_____
_____
_____
_____
_____
_____

◆ ◆ ◆ ◆ ◆

UNIT 7

THE PRE-OPENING

t this point in your workbook, you are well aware of the financials of opening a restaurant, hiring staff, and building a successful concept. Now that you have built a solid and organized business plan, found your space, and determined the best path of marketing, it is *time to work towards the opening of your restaurant.* In other words, it is time to take care of the **Pre-Opening tasks**.

There are a number of important tasks to complete before you open your restaurant. First, you need to decorate your restaurant, then purchase chairs, tables, lamps and other hardware. You need to make sure the kitchen has been correctly fitted out with the proper cooking equipment, and you need to purchase your Point of Sales system. It is a good idea to constantly check on the status of your permits and it is important to begin the process of navigating your first inventory ordering lists.

This Unit looks at planning for what you will face during the pre-opening, as well as help you organize the process in a clear and concise manner. Remember: each restaurant tends to have a unique set of pre-opening tasks to complete, so, in the Exercises, consider *how your concept applies* to the foundations discussed here.

Deco and refurbishments/Buying Essential Equipment

Once you find your restaurant space and sign your lease, the next step is to **furbish the space as needed,** with permission from the landlord. Good to discuss repairs and construction plans *before you sign your lease.*

So, first, *judge what needs to be done.* Make a list, and assign a level of complexity for each task, from painting to adding an extra bathroom. Some restaurateurs **hire a contractor** to manage the construction of their restaurant; you really should, if there is any major construction involved. Think about the **water and electric needs** of the space, including water and drainage lines added to all sinks behind the kitchen.

After construction, ***furbish the walls and floors***. This includes mirrors, paintings, advertisements or pieces of flair to your walls. Also, *lighting*. Some ***hire an interior designer.***

Once the walls and décor have been completed, ***turn to the table and chairs*** for your restaurant. Placement and size are critical, so make sure to spend time walking around the dining room to gauge the relationship of comfort to profit.

The *style of chair* is very important to the guest experience, unless you are opening a quick service restaurant; then the quality of the chair is less important. Plastic chairs tend to work well in quick service restaurants since they are easy to

In quick service restaurants, the tables should be easy to clean and durable. Style is not terribly important, either, but you need to make sure the table stands up to abuse over the long run. Most fine dining restaurants cover their tables with linens, so the appearance of the table itself is not very important. The table tends to be polished wood, but be sure to invest in high quality linens to cover your table.

Also consider any additional pieces of furniture you plan to include in your restaurant. For instance, you may need to put a waiter's station in the dining room; where will that go? What about waste paper baskets and bins? The placement of Point of Sales systems, entry ways and exits? Make sure to spend time thinking of each and every possibility when it comes to furbishing your space.

During the opening process, one of the most expensive and important ***purchases you will make involves equipment***. Most of the equipment you buy will be used in and by the kitchen, but you'll likely need equipment for your bar, as well. Be sure you can fit the equipment you buy in your space, and that you have purchased enough equipment to sustain your day to day business.

The first piece of equipment you are likely to buy is the **walk-in refrigerator**. It requires a large, flat space that is dry and not prone to flooding. The compressor tends to give off a lot of heat in the form of hot air; many restaurants place the compressor on the outside of the building to eliminate this added heat, but that depends on your city rules.

Smallwares, Glassware, Dishes and Silverware

As the construction phase carries on, it is important to buy the smallwares for your kitchen. ***Smallwares*** refer to the pots, pans, whisks, spatulas as well as the hundreds of other required pieces of equipment. As you determine the style of restaurant as well as the menu you plan on serving, you can begin the process of putting this list together. To make sure you do not buy too many items or buy the wrong items, it is always a good idea to have the chef manage the smallwares process.

One of the most time consuming components of the opening will be the time you spend buying **glassware, dishes** and **silverware**. While it might seem like a simple task, the sheer size and variety of potential solutions will take time to absorb

Before you start looking, make sure to *do a thorough inventory* in terms of needed items. For instance, if you have a restaurant with 75 seats, it's a good idea to order 100 plates of each type needed. While you might not use all the plates at once, remember that you will lose a plate or two from time to time due to wear and unexpected breaks. Pay attention to the per-item price. See where you can eliminate plates, glasses and silverware that are both above and below your budget.

It is important to buy plates, glasses and silverware that are durable and can withstand the chaotic environment of a professional kitchen. People will be able to recognise cheap plates, which can cheapen the perception of your restaurant. With this said, the most expensive plates (over £100 per plate) are the easiest ones to break. Your goal is the find a style and size of plate which balances quality and price. For this reason, it tends to take a lot of time to find the correct plates.

Once you choose the plates, glasses and silverware for your restaurant, it is a good idea to calculate the final cost. Many times, discounts are given if you buy a certain amount of plates, glasses and silverware. Discounts are typically larger for restaurants who buy their smallwares from the same company. Beyond discounts, ask yourself if you really need all the plates, glasses and silverware up front.

◆◆◆◆◆

MY RESTAURANT DESIGN, DÉCOR, SMALLWARES & FURBISHING NOTES & IDEAS

Feel free to Add notes on Glassware, Plates & Silver as Photos in the back of your Workbook!

_____
_____
_____
_____
_____
_____
_____
_____
_____
_____
_____
_____
_____
_____

_____

_____

_____

_____

◆ ◆ ◆ ◆ ◆

Permits and Licences

Permits and licensing depends on the local environment, so it is important to contact your local council or government to determine which permits are relevant to your business. While most people understand the need for a health and safety permit, many people might not be aware of the lesser permit requirements. For instance, your local town might require a permit for rubbish collection.

Here is a short checklist of potential permits & licenses to open and run your restaurant. Do your research and create your own in the next Exercise.

✓ The first permit you are likely to encounter when opening a restaurant involves the **formation of the business**. Whether you form an LLC or incorporate, the very action of starting a company in many ways is a permit.

✓ Next, apply for a permit related to the **collection of taxes**. In many areas, the local government allows the restaurant to collect taxes on their behalf. You should contact your local government tax department to decide which type of taxes you need to collect and how you remit this money

✓ The most important permit you need involves the health and safety of your customers. Many localities will require you to get **a certificate of occupancy**, a process which covers the safety of the physical space.

✓ The most confusing and stressful permit you will need to get involves the **local Department of Health**; it allows you to legally sell foods to the public and typically requires an on-site inspection. Often, the local health department will provide you with _written guidelines_ in order to successfully pass your initial inspection. Follow this material closely.

✓ The next permit you will need is your **liquor license**, to serve alcohol at the restaurant. The is probably the most time consuming and stressful permit of a restaurant's opening.

✓ Many local councils require you to obtain **a permit for waste removal**.

✓ Other localities require **permitting for the frontage** of your restaurant.

Once you have all of your permits, be sure to _**schedule calling in your Compliance Inspectors**_ as you lead up to your Opening.

◆◆◆◆◆

Contact your local government and research all the potential permits you need. List them including estimated time to acquire in the space below.

_____

_____

_____

_____

_____

_____

_____

_____

_____

_____

_____

_____

_____

_____

_____

_____

_____

_____

_____

_____

_____

_____

_____

_____

_____

_____

_____

_____

_____

_____

_____

_____

_____

_____

_____

_____

_____

_____
_____
_____
_____
_____
_____
_____
_____
_____
_____
_____
_____
_____
_____
_____
_____
_____

◆ ◆ ◆ ◆ ◆

Point of Sales System (POS) & Credit Card Processing

During the pre-opening process, it is a good idea to spend a lot of time looking into **Point of Sales systems**. A point of sales system is your way of creating receipts, informing the kitchen of orders as well as getting a sense of your financial numbers. Purchasing the correct POS system is important to your long term success, which is why we will spend a bit of time discussing the functions of a POS system in a restaurant.

Beyond organizing and delegating orders, the POS system prints the receipts and bills you hand to your customers. Many POS systems include a credit card swiper to help with the billing process. It is always a good idea to purchase a manual method for writing invoices, order and recording credit card receipts just in case your POS goes down during a busy service. Perhaps the greatest tools in your POS relate to the ways in which you can study the financials of your operation

In the modern world, most of restaurant transactions are conducted through credit and debit cards. For this reason, it is extremely important to set up a merchant account with a credit/debit card processing company. Many companies will supply you with the processor for free. Instead, the processing companies make money by charging you a certain percent of each transaction. This amount is automatically deducted from the transaction balance of each day. Most credit card companies transfer the funds to your account within three days of the transaction

Initial Stocking

When ordering your initial supplies, it is a good idea to start by *ordering in terms of shelf life*. Try and list your inventory lists in terms of dry goods and perishables then apply this specialized list to your initial ordering day. The first supplies you want to order involve the **cleaning supplies**. Paper napkins, plates, cups, soap, paper towels, toilet paper, bleach and ammonia, to name a few supplies; you can easily store them weeks before the opening.

Next is the **dry goods** of the restaurant. These food goods can last for weeks or months as well, but you definitely want to wait till after the construction of the kitchen and restaurant is complete before ordering any food goods. You also need to *make sure that your kitchen smallwares have arrived* for the restaurant before you order dry goods. If you order dry goods and do not have any containers to put the inventory in, you might have a difficult day! Dry goods include flour, sugar, coffee, ketchup, canned goods, salt, pepper, spices, pasta and such. For the first month of the opening, you do not want to spend a lot of time chasing down small, inexpensive dry goods, so *make sure to order a large supply* of guest sugar packets, straws, etc., in order to assure you do not run out of crucial supplies.

Once you obtain the liquor license, you can begin to **bring your booze** to the restaurant. Call your liquor suppliers and have them make their deliveries. Once again, you want to make sure your construction phase is finished by this point; it is important to limit access to the alcohol when it arrives at the restaurant.

Now that you have your cleaning supplies, alcohol and dry goods, it is time to turn to your **perishable goods**. Perishable goods are foods with a rather rapid expiration date. Since they spoil quickly, you want to order these goods the day before you open the restaurant. With this said, your chef might want to prepare a few things a week before the opening of the restaurant. Because of this, you might need to order bones, onion, celer,y and carrots a week before the opening. Ask the chef to manage the intake of perishable goods.

The day of the opening is the day you want to receive **highly perishable items**. For instance, it is a good idea to order the fish and herbs on the first day you are open. Make sure to keep the foods fresh by not getting too far ahead when it comes to ordering your initial inventory.

Choosing an Opening Date

One of the most unpredictable tasks you have to master during the pre-opening involves **picking the opening date**. It is important to choose an opening date early in the process to organize your marketing strategy and advertising campaigns. It is very difficult to correctly guess your opening date, especially when you are dealing with construction and supply issues. For this reason, you will need to hold off on choosing an opening date until the correct time.

The correct time to *declare your opening date is about two weeks before* you open. This gives you enough time to contact the health inspector to plan an inspection date. Two weeks will give you enough time to order supplies, hire staff and train them as needed. To make this process easier, it is important to *have your marketing and advertising plan mapped ou*t before you pull the trigger.

As the day of the opening nears, you can implement your online marketing scheme. Social media is perhaps the most powerful form of marketing today, so creating a well thought-out marketing plan can significantly increase your restaurant's reach. Social media also tends to be cheaper than print media, although it requires a clever approach.

As you approach the opening, create photos of your space and menu items to add to your website and social media accounts. Weeks before the restaurant is due to open, start accounts for Facebook, Twitter, and Instagram, as well as any additional sites you feel will work well for your business. Ask your friends to register a "like" on your new restaurant page, and offer them a discount for coming to your restaurant. Start following people on Twitter who live in your local area to target customers. Post pleasing photos to Instagram of your space and food. Beyond this, you want to build a long term audience. Offer specials whenever possible, and make sure to advertise special meals and events.

◆◆◆◆◆

EXERCISE: BUILD A PRE-OPENING TIMELINE

There is so much to plan and consider. But, based on your work in this chapter, use the Exercise below to build a Timeline Checklist of pre-opening purchases, inspections, final hires, and social media blasts starting two months out down to the day of your Big Opening!

TWO MONTHS PRE-OPENING

_____
_____
_____
_____
_____
_____
_____

_____
_____
_____
_____
_____
_____
_____
_____

SIX-WEEKS PRE-OPENING

_____
_____
_____
_____
_____
_____
_____
_____
_____
_____
_____
_____
_____
_____
_____

ONE MONTH PRE-OPENING

_____
_____
_____
_____
_____
_____
_____
_____

_____
_____
_____
_____
_____
_____
_____
_____

THREE WEEKS PRE-OPENING

_____
_____
_____
_____
_____
_____
_____
_____
_____
_____
_____
_____
_____
_____
_____
_____
_____

TWO WEEKS PRE-OPENING:

_____
_____
_____
_____
_____
_____
_____
_____
_____
_____
_____
_____

_____

_____

_____

_____

_____

_____

ONE WEEK PRE-OPENING:

_____

_____

_____

_____

_____

_____

_____

_____

_____

_____

_____

_____

_____

_____

_____

_____

FIVE DAYS PRE-OPENING

_____

_____

_____

_____

_____

_____

_____

_____

_____

_____

_____

_____

_____

_____
_____
_____
_____
_____

FOUR DAYS PRE-OPENING

_____
_____
_____
_____
_____
_____
_____
_____
_____
_____
_____
_____
_____
_____
_____
_____

THREE DAYS PRE-OPENING (Don't forget your front/back of house staff Mixer!)

_____
_____
_____
_____
_____
_____
_____
_____
_____
_____
_____
_____
_____
_____
_____

TWO DAYS PRE-OPENING

DAY BEFORE OPENING!

◆ ◆ ◆ ◆ ◆

UNIT 8

THE OPENING

The opening of your restaurant can be a stressful or exciting process. If you have followed the steps listed in this workbook, your experience will most likely be stress-free. Remember: the key to a smooth opening is organization. It is important to constantly organize and reorganize yourself.

When you are ready to open the doors, there are a few final and important tasks to complete in order to steer your business in the correct direction. During the opening, you are sure to run into a few kinks, so finding these errors and offering solutions are very important.

The Friends/Family Test Run

Before you open your doors to the public, it is a good idea to celebrate your accomplishment by inviting family and friends to dinner. Being the first meal you serve, the formality should always be low, and mistakes should be forgiven quickly. This **pre-opening night** allows the kitchen crew and front of house staff to become comfortable with the restaurant and procedures. The staff will observe obstacles and find solutions to these obstacles. The test run involving your family and friends should happen *the night before you open the doors*. This will allow you to minimize the expenses related to the party.

When serving a family and friend test run, it is customary to not charge your guests. Instead, you should invite your guests to enjoy the restaurant and menu without high expectations. Besides, if you invite 75 people to your test run, you will have 75 people talking about your restaurant before it opens, which is a great addition to your early marketing plan.

To reduce the cost of your test run, consider serving a set menu along with some of the cheaper wines offered at the restaurant. Make sure to ask your guests what they think of the food and service. If their suggestions are good, try and implement them into your procedures and recipes. At the end of the party, discuss with the staff the complexities of the night. Listen to their suggestions and implement plans that are useful and solve problems.

◆◆◆◆◆

EXERCISE: ADD YOUR TEST RUN TO THE TIMELINE IN UNIT 7, INCLUDING INVITATIONS, ETC.

◆◆◆◆◆

Day 1

Opening day will be busy no matter how organized you are, and you are unlikely to get a lot of sleep the night before you open the doors. You will be working very long hours and will have to interact with guests from the perspective of a restaurant owner. The best advice I can give you is to enjoy the day and take things as they come!

Depending on the opening time of your restaurant, you will need to arrive early. If your restaurant opens at 8 a.m., it is a good idea to get to the restaurant at *least two hours earlier*. With the extra time, complete a final review of all your procedures. Test all of the essential equipment, making sure all of the key staff members are ready for the day, and the supplies are completely stocked. If you are organized early, open the doors fifteen minutes before 8 a. m. Sometimes it's nice to know you are ahead of schedule.

If your restaurant opens at six in the evening, try *to get to the restaurant at noon*. This will give you time to call people during business hours, receive orders and review procedures. If you are open from 8 a.m. to midnight, it will be difficult for you to spend the entire sixteen hours on your feet. For this reason, you might want to *schedule an hour or two break in the afternoon*. Remember to manage your own working hours with the working hours of the restaurant. As you settle into the business, you can start to sleep more as needed.

As your first guests arrive, make sure to not smother them or stare. Since this is your first customer, your energy and excitement will be quite high. Give them the normal amount of service and attention, and mention to them at the end of the meal that they are table number one. Make sure to keep the first bill you make!

As the diners enjoy your restaurant throughout the day, *observe your staff* and make adjustments as necessary.

Not all your opening tasks relate to the front of house. Instead, it is a good idea to spend a bit of time in the kitchen to observe the procedures and flow of a dinner service, just not when it's very busy. This can be a very fun experience. Make sure to *get to know the kitchen staff*.

As you make your way through the first day of business, you might be tempted to have a few drinks and mingle with the crowd. It is never a good idea to drink during the day, even if you are the owner. Make sure to *save your own relaxation time for the end of the night*.

Then, spend time contemplating the day. You have worked hard to get to that point, so make sure you continue your work hard. Spend a few hours thinking of specific events, interesting financials and future concepts you would like to implement into your business.

◆◆◆◆◆

MY OPENING DAY SCHEDULE

You may be opening your Dream Restaurant very soon or it may be a long ways off. But at this point in your workbook, you have an idea of what sort of restaurant you envision and what its hours will be, how you will prepare for your Opening Day, and what it will be like when it comes.

This is a creative essay for you to dream about that day in concrete terms, starting with the ring of your alarm clock. Walk yourself through the day, see who you will greet, what you'll observe, how you will manage with your GM and Chef to serve great food, what you'll do to wrap out your evening, and then how you'll relax and unwind with colleagues and family. It might not happen *exactly* like this, but this Exercise may help more of it come true! *If you can believe it, you can do it!*

_____
_____
_____
_____
_____
_____
_____
_____
_____
_____
_____
_____
_____
_____
_____

◆ ◆ ◆ ◆ ◆

Week One

As the end of week one approaches, you will be quite familiar with your staff and you will have worked out most of the kinks in your operation. You have served a lot of guests and observed a lot of great financial insight through your point of sales system. With this said, there are a number of events you might encounter during week one which are worthy of discussion.

➢ It is a good idea to remember you **might face an inspection** during the first week which is outside the bounds of the health department. The local tax collector or liquor authority might stop by.

➢ A **member of the press** might stop by incognito to get a sense of your restaurant, so treat every guest as if they were a big time food reviewer.

➢ You are likely to **receive food orders** during the course of the week. Fish typically arrives on a daily basis, while you will have received goods from the meat company two or three times. You will have received a produce order every day, linen orders, dry goods, and so on. In a few days, you can have a staggering number of invoices. It is important to **keep these invoices and prepare to send payments to the suppliers**.

➢ As with statistics, the larger the sample the better the **information you can extract from the data.** Hundreds of customers helps, and thousands of customers give you a clearer sense of your business. Once you complete your first week, you will have a large amount of data, and a clearer sense of your business model will begin to develop. **Make sure to study your data in great depth during the first week.**

➢ By the end of week one, you should have **solved 99% percent of the problems related to the kitchen and service**.

Month One

As month one nears an end, your data set has increased greatly and you have solved nearly every problem you might encounter. By month one, you are sure to have **lost an employee or two**, and the stars of the **staff are starting to demonstrate leadership qualitie**s. While you might not be turning a profit at the one month mark, it is important to **study your financials in detail**.

The best way to study your financials is to **compare them to your business plan.** Study the business plan and determine *which goals have been met* and *which goals still need work*. **Report** on how your opening cost estimates compared to the actual costs of the opening and month one. Compile your data into a report and **share this information with your investors**. By offering a detailed review after month one, you are demonstrating your ability to run the business. In many ways, this quality is more important at the one month mark than the profit/loss statement.

At the end of the first month, it is a good idea to ***review your marketing strategy***. Ask yourself which strategy worked best and pour your budget and resources into this channel

If you plan on ***expanding your operating hours*** after the first month, remember that you will need to *hire extra staff* beforehand. Luckily, you will already have a number of competent, highly trained employees to help teach the newly hired.

The first month of business will be full of long hours and stressful moments. For this reason, it's a good idea to ***take a break towards the end of the first month***. Make sure to catch up on lost sleep and take a mini-holiday if needed.

◆◆◆◆◆

MY FIRST MONTH CHECKLIST

Review the Workbook notes for Opening, Week One and Month One above. Compile a checklist for yourself that you can revisit as your restaurant comes to fruition. Add to it during your planning and preparation period but then be sure to check in and run it when that first day and month arrive!

MY FIRST DAY-WEEK-MONTH CHECKLIST

✓ _____
✓ _____
✓ _____
✓ _____
✓ _____
✓ _____
✓ _____
✓ _____
✓ _____
✓ _____
✓ _____
✓ _____
✓ _____
✓ _____
✓ _____
✓ _____

✓ _____

✓ _____

✓ _____

✓ _____

✓ _____

✓ _____

◆◆◆◆◆

Month Three

The three-month mark after opening your restaurant represents the first quarter of business. By this time, you will have built a loyal clientele and continue to attract new guests to your restaurant. The weekends tend to be very busy, while Tuesdays can seem a bit slow. You have adjusted your level of staff to account for this trend. As you move towards Day 100 of the business, you will have a great sense of your actual business model as well as the probability of running a successful business in the long run.

The note above which makes mention of the slow-Tuesday trend is important to pay attention to. It is imperative to **understand the most common days and hours that your restaurant is busy.** By doing so, you can **OPTIMIZE your labour schedule** by reducing staff on the slow days and increasing staff on the busy days. For instance, many kitchens set their off days for Sunday, Monday and Tuesday in order to reduce the labour cost of these slow days.

Beyond the labour schedule, a number of important trends have formed in your restaurant. For instance, you are sure to **have a couple dishes which clearly outsell other items** of the menu. These dishes might be mentioned by the press in local newspapers and media as standouts, and your customers are quite happy with the tastes of the select dishes as well. Because of their popularity, these should be considered **your signature dishes**. As you change your menu in the future, you *do not want leave signature items off* the menu.

For the first month or two of your restaurant operation, you might not make a profit. Your volumes will still be low and your staff will need time to reach the correct level of efficiency. Mistakes might be made in the kitchen which eats deeply into your potential profit margin. By month three, you should be able to **get a clear picture of your profit/loss potential.** Study your financials and determine which menu items have been successful and which ones are not. Study the profit margin for each. After three months, you might decide to eliminate a recipe or wine. At month three, it is time to make financial sense of your restaurant.

How to Remain "New" Beyond the Opening

As a restaurant passes its opening quarter, the restaurant will still seem new to your local audience. With this said, it is important to keep in mind **your operation is becoming older and less relevant** in terms of the local, everyday conversation. To constantly bring in new business, it is important to remain fresh in the consumers' minds. For instance, you might decide to **change the menu seasonally** in order to share the fresh update with your current and potential customers. This gives you the opportunity to reach new clients and customers you have already served.

If you offer music or entertainment during the evening, **hiring new bands and providing new types of music** is a great way to stay new. Many restaurants, especially casual ones, include **a social night or two** during the week, like a food trivia night, giving a gift certificate to the winner, or showing a movie during a casual night, including a karaoke night, etc..

To remain 'new', it is important to **perform daily maintenance to your restaurant**. A restaurant that is not cleaned daily or has obvious signs of wear and tear will not seem new, no matter how compelling the marketing strategy. In the first few months, this might include simple tasks like *washing the floor* and *dusting the walls*. As your restaurant ages, table might become off-centred and plates might be chipped. Take care of these issues quickly if you want to retain that new restaurant feel.

◆◆◆◆◆

MY IDEAS FOR STAYING "NEW"

This list will grow based on your specific restaurant and what happens in your first few months. But some will strike you as good ideas to implement down the road; others are things you want to put in place up front to keep your place fresh and inviting. Start your list below!

_____

_____

_____

_____

_____

_____

_____

_____

_____

UNIT 9

THE NUMBERS OF RESTAURANT SUCCESS

So far, we have discussed creating a business plan and monitoring the financials of your restaurant. Since you are entering the restaurant business to make money, there is little need to explain why having a firm grasp on your financials is so important. However, we have not discussed the ***details of calculating the important financial measure*** of your restaurant.

As you can imagine, there are a number of ways to calculate the major values of your business. For instance, you can calculate your food cost in terms of each dish, or you can study the kitchen invoices versus total revenue. It is important to **choose a method of calculation** which makes sense for your business model. Hopefully, the following methods will help you create the most compelling and useful way to display your food calculations.

Calculating Food Cost

Before you calculate the cost of food, it is important to keep a few points in mind.

> ➤ First, make sure you use the ***same dates for both revenue and invoices***. If you end up using invoices for thirty-five days and the revenue statement for thirty days, your food cost will be dramatically inaccurate.
> ➤ To calculate food cost, you will need to have a great sense of current inventory. For this reason, you will need to ***record your inventory at the conclusion of every night***.

To correctly calculate food cost, try the following method:

1. Determine Beginning Inventory (inventory from day before target dates)

2. Calculate the total cost of Purchases

3. Determine Ending Inventory (inventory from the last target date)

4. Determine Total Food Sales

Once you have this data, you can calculate your food cost thus:

Food Cost = <u>(Beginning Inventory + Purchases) - End Inventory</u>
<u>Food Sales</u>

Put another way: Food cost equals the *sum* of your Beginning inventory *plus* your purchases, then *subtract* your end inventory. *Divide* that number by the amount of food sales.

Here's a practical example:

Beginning Inventory = **£**100,000

Purchases = **£**20,000

Ending Inventory = **£**105,000

Total Food Sales = **£**50,000

So, plugged into our formula:

Food Cost = <u>(£100,000 + £20,000) - £105,000</u>

£50,000

Food Cost = <u>£15,000</u>
£50,000

Food Cost = 0.3 x 100%

<u>Food Cost = 30%</u>

◆◆◆◆◆◆

FOOD COST EXERCISE

TRY ONE ON YOUR OWN WITH THE FOLLOWING DATA:

Your Restaurant's Beginning Inventory = £75,000

Purchases = £12,000

Ending Inventory = £80,000

Total Food Sales = £40,000

Do your Own Calculations following my Model in the Space Below:

_____
_____
_____
_____
_____
_____
_____
_____
_____
_____
_____
_____
_____
_____
_____
_____
_____
_____
_____

◆◆◆◆◆

Controlling Labour Cost

Besides food cost, the **cost of labour** will be one of your largest expenses. For this reason, it is important to get a great sense of your cost of labour. As we discussed before, you want to minimize labour on slow days and maximize labour on busy days. With this said, it is still important to control your labour costs in a more mathematical way.

To gain the most useful sense of your labour costs, try applying the following method:

1. Divide your employees into categories. Categories should reflect the pay grade (salary) for each employee type. For instance, the Maitre D. and Executive Chef will be the highest salaries, while the kitchen assistants and general cleaners will have the lowest salaries. All employees who receive the same pay or salary should be included in the same group.

2. Add the total number of work hours for each pay category. For example, if you have 5 employees who earn £10 an hour and work 30 hours each, the total number of hours worked will be 150 hours.

3. Multiply the hourly rate by the total number of hours. Using the example above, you can quickly determine that the total wage will be £1,500.

4. Determine the weekly rate for salaried employees. For instance, if you pay a manager £52,000 a year, the weekly salary would be £1,000.

5. Add the wages of each pay group together in terms of weekly rates. This will give you a sense of your total labour cost per week.

COST OF LABOR EXERCISE

PAY GRADES	AMOUNT/HR	# of WORKERS @ RATE	# of HRS/WK	TOTAL WAGE (Hrly rate x total # of hrs)

LABOR COST/WEEK (TOTAL OF ALL WAGES) _____

◆◆◆◆◆

How to Price Your Menu Items

Once you settle into your restaurant, you will gain a great sense of which dishes are popular and which dishes are not. You can compare the profit margin of each dish to determine your long term menu success. It is important to *maintain recipes which prove quite popular and profitable*. You might want to *dump menu items which are not profitable and do not sell*. These items can be quite detrimental to your bottom line.

In terms of items which do not sell, the largest loss is to your profit margin. To prepare these dishes, you will have to order foods that are perishable, so which have an expiration date. If the food sits in your kitchen and needs to be thrown out due to spoiling, this will dramatically impact your profit margin. Instead, lose dishes which are not popular and replace them with dishes which are popular. Not only will you save money on perishable foods, you can dramatically increase the number of customers who come to your restaurant.

Some strategies to keep in mind:

✓ You can *increase the price of the dish* that is popular and not profitable. It is never a good idea to increase the price by 10%.

✓ If you need to trim the cost of the recipe, you can *reducing the size of the portion.*

✓ Additionally, you can *change the most expensive ingredient* in the recipe.

Beyond the food, you should **review the prices you are charging at the bar.**

✓ Perhaps a drink takes too long to make, which can increase your labour cost. Find a solution to *make the drink quicker.*

✓ Sometimes, the ingredients are too expensive. Make the change as soon as possible.

✓ Discuss the prices of your goods with your wine and alcohol suppliers. These companies are often flexible with their prices, so make sure to *ask for discounts and rebates.*

✓ Another place where prices can get out of whack behind the bar deals with portioning. *Learn to correctly portion the liquor;* make sure your bartenders are well aware of the correct way to portion liquor. This will help you correctly price your menu.

When pricing a menu after you open, the art is less in the actual pricing and more in the realm of **finding backend solutions**. Backend solutions include correctly portioning foods and beverages, finding cheaper ingredients, and so on. Changing the prices in front of a consumer can be tricky, especially when you are a young restaurant. For this reason, **changing prices should be seen as a last resort** to make your profit margin. By finding the correct balance when it comes to pricing your menu beyond the opening, success will be much easier to attain.

◆◆◆◆◆

PRICING EXERCISE

Revisit 3-6 items on your Draft Menu in Unit 6—starters, main, desserts, cocktails—and do a little research on material costs to calculate some good initial prices. **Check back on the Unit 6 pricing Formula.** Describe them in the space below. Use this worksheet to compare with comparable restaurants in your area, as you visit them during your restaurant development. Where might you find savings or other Backend solutions to increase profit margins?

Menu Item 1:

_____

_____

Ingredients & Food costs list

_____

_____

_____

_____

_____

_____

_____

_____

_____

_____

Starting Price _____

Menu Item 2:

_____

_____

Ingredients & Food costs list

_____

_____

_____

_____

_____

_____

_____
_____
_____
_____

Starting Price _____

Menu Item 3:

_____
_____

Ingredients & Food costs list

_____
_____
_____
_____
_____
_____
_____
_____
_____
_____

Starting Price _____

Menu Item 4:

_____
_____

Ingredients & Food costs list

_____
_____
_____
_____
_____
_____
_____
_____
_____

Starting Price _____

Menu Item 5:

_____
_____

Ingredients & Food costs list

_____
_____
_____
_____
_____
_____
_____
_____
_____
_____
_____
_____

Starting Price _____

Menu Item 6:

_____
_____

Ingredients & Food costs list

_____
_____
_____
_____
_____
_____
_____
_____
_____
_____
_____
_____

Starting Price _____

◆ ◆ ◆ ◆ ◆

UNIT 10

HOW TO BUILD A LOYAL CLIENTELE

In order to become a successful restaurant, it is imperative to build a loyal clientele. By far the most effective way of building a loyal clientele is by ***serving a high quality, consistent product***. If you serve a meal with a higher degree of quality, you are sure to stand out among your competition. In time, restaurant customers tend to migrate to restaurants that serve high quality fare.

Beyond quality, there are a number of additional tricks you can employ to build a loyal restaurant clientele like giving your guests the VIP treatment each time they dine in your restaurant; loyalty cards, carrying free meals and other promotions will also help to draw customer back. As always, social media is a powerful tool for building a constant message in the consumers mind. Other techniques include going off the menu.

This Unit looks at some of these basic devices for building and keeping your clientele.

Quality

By far, the most important strategy to build a long-term, loyal customer base is to **serve a high quality meal**. You might serve nine wonderful meals to a particular client, only to serve a less than stellar meal on the tenth try. While you did a great job nine times in a row, the tenth attempt caused you to lose a loyal customer. Do this a couple hundred times, and you will quickly be out of business... For this reason, remember to maintain a high quality meal.

It is easy to say "serve a high quality meal," but understanding may be a different story. For example, let's say you have opening a new sandwich shop with a very clean and concise menu, brand, and atmosphere. You make great bread and serve artisanal meats. Yet your lettuce tends to wilt in the sandwich display. A customer comes to your restaurant and is served a sandwich with the sub-par lettuce. He gets sick from the lettuce, vows to never come back, and tells his friends.

Or say you have a beautiful new fine dining restaurant with great service. A loyal customer comes once a week for his favourite steak. While the quality of your meat is extraordinary, what if your new cook keeps overcooking the £100 steak. The loyal customer will no longer show up on Tuesday night.

While you might consider 99% of the quality issues of your restaurant, neglecting the 1% can have disastrous consequences. This is especially true over time.

In order to maintain a quality meal, it is best to first **start at the door**. Every once in a while, make sure to discuss with the chef the *performance of your suppliers*. If a supplier is consistently giving you low quality foods, consider finding an alternative. From here, make sure the *chef does not order too much* on the inventory. Ordering too much will cause you to serve lower quality meals as well as increase your food cost. Finally, make sure you *test the food all the time*. Order a dish from the kitchen and make sure it is of the standard you have set forward with the kitchen.

Beyond quality food, you need to make sure you **continue to serve a high quality meal.** Not in terms of the food, but in terms of the service. The front of the house should always *remain clean and organized*, and the service *staff should always remain attentive*. Once you see waiters checking their mobile phones in the middle of a busy service, it is time to complete a quality assessment. Beyond the behaviour of the waiting staff, make sure the *bar section of your restaurant continues to serve the same quality drinks*. If you are going through a lot of bar staff, make sure the quality of the drinks has not shifted from the original creations to present. Remember, a complete commitment to quality will go a very long way.

Giving your Audience the VIP Treatment

There are two types of VIP treatment:

- ➢ The treatment you give to each and every guest (who should ALL be treated like VIPs)
- ➢ The treatment you give to loyal customers.

While it is important to *treat all guests as VIPs,* the people who bring you the most business deserve the most select and tailored service. For one, make sure to **remember the names of your loyal guests**, their **favourite drinks and food**. If your loyal customers come to your restaurant on an anniversary, for example, it's always a good idea to **write this information down in a calendar**. The next year they come to celebrate their favourite meal, being greeted for their special occasion will certainly make the night a bit more special.

Consider *buying your loyal guests a free drink* before the meal. Some restaurants lure loyal clients to their tables by *going off the menu*. For instance, if a repeat customer asks you to prepare a dish off the menu, it is always a good idea to say yes to his or her request.

A great way to build a loyal clientele is to **have your staff memorize the names of your VIPs.** For high frequency customers, **make sure to hold tables or make room for them on very busy nights**. While you will be ecstatic to serve a packed house, **never forget those who are most loyal** to you.

Loyalty Cards, Social Media Discounts

Loyalty Cards can be a great way to bring customers back to your restaurant. This is especially true when it comes to quick service and casual restaurants. There are a number of ways to market and study loyalty cards.

Many quick service and fast casual restaurants keep their loyalty cards rather secret. Instead of advertising and handing a card to every customer, the staff retain the cards and give them to customers whom they recognize as repeat customers. **Secret loyalty cards** make your loyal customers feel special, a task that is hard to manage when you serve thousands of meals a day. In terms of content, you might decide to *award your loyal customers points* in order to redeem free food or merchandise. Or, you might decide to take a more direct route. For instance, receive a *free meal on every tenth purchase*. Once again, make sure to study the needs and desires of your loyal customers before implementing loyalty cards.

Some food service establishments **advertise their loyalty cards**. For instance, the restaurant might charge £25 for a loyalty card, but offer a 5% discount on each and every purchase thereafter. While this might seem like an expensive proposition, gaining a loyal customer over time will make the 5% discount seem like a moot point.

Beyond keeping your frequent customers happy, a loyalty card gives you a tremendous amount of data in terms of repeat customers. By analyzing the data of each card, you can determine which time your repeat customers come to your restaurant, on which day, which items are popular with loyal customers, how much they spend, and what complimentary items they order

Fine dining restaurants rely on **recognizing the individual guests**. This starts when the guest calls the restaurant to make a reservation and extends to the behaviour of the staff. With this said, make sure to track the data of your loyal customers.

A great way to build a loyal clientele is to build a **robust social marketing campaign.** As the weekend nears and people start to make their dining plans, adding a discount within the social media realm can draw people to your restaurant.

The two largest sources of loyal customers from social media can be currently found through Facebook and Twitter. Both platforms can serve your restaurant in a number of ways, so identify which **Social Media Discount** techniques work well in your local area. To accomplish this, study your competition. Observe the Facebook and Twitter accounts of other restaurants to discover how they draw in crowds. Do *they* offer specials? Do *they* post new and unique menu item descriptions or photos? Do *they* promote the local football club? Do *they* recognize their loyal customers by mentioning them in twitter feeds? These are just a few questions you should consider when studying the competition.

Once you have studied the competition, the next step is to **put together your social media strategy to entice loyal customers**. Beyond the message, you need to get a good sense of the *most effective time and days* to promote your restaurant. For instance, if you plan on offering a promotion on Saturday night, Monday night might not be the best time to post your offer.

It is often difficult to judge how popular your social media campaigns end up being. Not every guest who comes to your restaurant will take you to the side to confirm your social media campaign brought them to your restaurant. Instead, you need to monitor social media yourself. Do people add your location to their Facebook feeds when dining out? Are you mentioned in any tweets? Find the best strategy to discover this information. In time, you will compile a comprehensive and effective social media strategy in order to build a loyal customer base.

Going off the menu

A great way to build a loyal clientele is to create menu items not listed on the menu. For instance, many quick service restaurants have found **secret menus** a great way to build a loyal and cult-like clientele. If you serve burgers, this process might include a special bacon variety or an extra-large burger. If you are a fine dining restaurant, the off-the-menu dish might be a new concoction the chef is trying out.

There are many ways to create a secret menu. Sometimes, a restaurants' secret menu will be **tailored to each guest**. For instance, if a guest constantly orders the same dish with the same modifications, you might consider naming the dish after the customer. Your loyal customer will be quite honoured with the listing.

For other restaurants, the secret menu is better known. The "secret" menu is **advertised in local media and social media** sites but not given to each guest who enters the restaurant. The customer has to *ask for the menu* to unlock the key.

The content of a secret menu can vary greatly. However, make sure to use as many ingredients as you can from the normal menu. If you have a number of unique dishes on the secret menu but no one asks for it for a few days, you will be in trouble in terms of food cost. Instead, *try and create a secret menu that makes use of one unique ingredient plus your current ingredient list*. Alternatively, try *increasing the portion size* when it comes to a secret menu item. Remember, secret menu items need to **be unique and provide a sense of value** which goes beyond the food on the plate.

Besides serving a secret menu, there are a number of ways to share off-the-menu items with your guests. If you are open for a holiday, try and serve the **traditional foods of the holiday.** For instance, if you are open on the day of the American Thanksgiving Holiday (last Thursday in November), try and serve a traditional Thanksgiving dinner. While it is hard to sell this meal on Thanksgiving in America (since everyone is eating at home), you might be surprised by the number of expats who come to your special meal. As always, promote the event through social media and other avenues when appropriate.

A common technique when it comes to serving meals not on the menu involves **daily specials.** Daily specials are a great way to sell foods that are reaching their expiration date. During the course of the business week, your suppliers will approach you with special deals. Paying close attention to these offerings, and creating specials based on these discounted foods can be a great way to fatten your bottom line.

Special Events and Promotions

Besides offering discounts through social media and loyalty cards, offering special events and promotions is a great way to build long term relationships in the restaurant business. Make sure to **ask your loyal customers what sort of special events** will be most attractive to them.

The first type of special event you might consider involves **holidays**. For instance, if you open a fine dining or casual restaurant, you might consider an exquisite New Year's Celebration. Besides the New Year, there are a number of great days to hold special events. These days tend to vary from country to country. Begin to plan the event early and market early to bring in the most loyal customers on such special evenings.

Many restaurants, especially casual ones, offer **promotions on a weekly basis**. For instance, restaurants with an appropriate setting do rather well when serving a Movie Night, a night with a meal themed around the movie being screened. Some restaurants find trivia to be a great way to bring new customers—music, pop culture, or, if your restaurant is a sports bar, trivia that sports-related.

There are other great themes to promote when holding a special event. If you live in a football centred town, it is always a great idea to hold a meal which **promotes the team or a charity of the team. Casino nights** are also a great idea for bar-centred restaurants.

As you grow your restaurant form year to year, you will learn which special events draw the largest crowds. Make sure to **stick with these concepts** and stay away from concepts which are less desirable to your audience.

◆◆◆◆◆

MY SPECIAL CLIENTELE BUILDING & APPRECIATION STRATEGY

Pulling from the many ideas presented in this Unit, note down some ideas that you think would work in your Dream Restaurant, what the details of that would be to fit your business plan, and when you might consider introducing or developing these techniques to attract loyal customers and keep them satisfied and engaged.

_____

_____

_____

_____

_____

_____

_____

_____

_____

_____

_____

_____

_____

_____

_____

_____

_____

_____

_____

_____

_____

_____

_____

_____

_____

CONCLUSION

BUSINESS PLAN WORKSHEET & SKETCHBOOK

Your head should be chock full of great ideas for planning, launching, or developing your restaurant and entry into the food service industry. There is plenty of time to do additional research and fill in the rest of your Workbook. But of key importance is that you develop or update your Business Plan so that you can make your dreams a reality!

Waaaaay back in Unit 1, we discussed the elements of your Business Plan and you began to develop this important foundation for your Restaurant business. This Conclusion Unit gives you space to bring together elements and information you have learned and gathered throughout the Workbook to build your actual Business Plan. It is also a space to sketch, tape, glue, staple creative ideas and elements for your restaurant as you discover them. You should also have a computer folder where you can stash sample designs and colors, furniture and plate designs, menu ideas and anything else you discover in your restaurant development so they are there when you need to make some decisions!

◆◆◆◆◆

BUSINESS PLAN

INTRODUCTION: EXECUTIVE SUMMARY

1. Legal Arrangement of Business:

Describe the legal structure of ownership and responsibility (e.g., LLC, S-Corp, etc.):

_____

_____

_____

_____

_____

_____

2. Restaurant Lease or Purchase

_____

_____

_____

_____

3. Capitalization needs.

_____

_____

_____

_____

_____

_____

_____

_____

_____

_____

_____

_____

_____

_____

_____

_____

_____

_____

_____

_____

_____

_____

_____

_____

_____

4. Business Concept

Present a convincing argument as to why your restaurant idea will be more successful than others with passion, painting a descriptive picture of your goals.

_____
_____
_____
_____
_____
_____
_____
_____
_____
_____
_____
_____
_____
_____
_____
_____
_____
_____
_____
_____
_____
_____
_____
_____
_____

5. Sample menu

Refer back to Unit 6 to add details here that will help attract investors through their stomachs. Include prices and showcase the style of food you plan on selling. Formal restaurants will have lengthy and descriptive menus while fast casual restaurant menus will be short and to the point.

_____
_____
_____
_____
_____
_____
_____
_____
_____
_____
_____
_____
_____
_____
_____
_____
_____
_____
_____
_____
_____
_____
_____
_____
_____
_____
_____
_____

6. Restaurant Design and Layout

_____
_____
_____
_____
_____
_____
_____
_____

7. Restaurant Management Team Overview

For this section, collect and include the following elements for your management team overview:

- o Management Organizational Chart
- o CVs and Biographies of Managers
- o Management Contracts for the Restaurant
- o Financial Incentives for Managers

_____

_____

_____

_____

_____

_____

_____

_____

_____

_____

_____

_____

_____

_____

_____

_____

_____

_____

_____

_____

_____

_____

_____

_____

_____

_____

_____

_____

_____

_____

_____
_____
_____
_____
_____
_____
_____
_____
_____
_____
_____
_____
_____
_____
_____
_____
_____
_____

8. Restaurant Environment Analysis

Describes the competitive landscape of your market, including:

o   Study Restaurant Trends and Consumer Habits
o   Identify your Target Market
o   Location Analysis
o   Competitive Analysis

_____
_____
_____
_____
_____
_____
_____
_____
_____
_____
_____
_____
_____
_____

_____
_____
_____
_____
_____
_____
_____
_____
_____
_____
_____
_____
_____
_____
_____
_____
_____
_____
_____
_____
_____
_____
_____
_____
_____

9. Restaurant Marketing Strategy

Paint a picture of your strategy for **before** and **after** the opening. Make sure to distinguish these two marketing goals. Some great ways to build a compelling marketing strategy include:

- o Build a Customer Database for Direct Marketing
- o Create a Frequent Diner and VIP Programme
- o Develop a Compelling Email Campaign
- o Promote a Direct Mail Campaign for Your Local Postcode
- o Community Involvement such as Charity Events

- o Create T-shirts, Hats, Bumper Stickers, Business Cards
- o Hire a Public Relations Firm for Media Outreach
- o Include an Advertising Budget

_____

_____

_____

_____

_____

_____

_____

10. Restaurant Operations Plan

The operations plan within your business plan is the largest section of the document and conveys the general day-to-day aspects of your operation. Include:Staff Structure

- Employee Training Manual
- Suppliers
- Management Controls
- Point of Sales System
- Expected Labour Schedule
- Time and Attendance Tracking
- Inventory Control Method
- Insurance and Liability Controls
- Administrative Controls
- Cash Controls
- Weekly Profit/Loss Statement
- Method of Bookkeeping
- Payroll Processing

_____

_____

_____

_____

_____

_____

_____

_____

_____

_____

_____

_____

_____

_____

_____

_____

_____

_____

_____

♦ ♦ ♦ ♦ ♦

MY SKETCHES, COLORS, SCRAPBOOK, DESIGNS—PASTE/STAPLE THEM HERE!

SKETCHES, COLORS, SCRAPBOOK, DESIGNS

SKETCHES, COLORS, SCRAPBOOK, DESIGNS

ABOUT CHARLES

Charles Okwalinga entered the restaurant business along with his supportive wife, Margaret, when they opened their first restaurant, Exceline, in London UK in 2003. Margaret, trained in Catering and Hotel Management and a very creative recipe formulator, partnered with Charles in founding their restaurant, a fine dining African Restaurant concept.

Being passionate in business development and customer services, Charles learned his experience, passion and diligence in running the restaurant that has stood in consistency and quality for ten years, a success uncommon in the industry.

In running Exceline, Charles now has taken the knowledge, skills, and experience in the industry and written his book *A Recipe for Restaurant Success* and additional available materials to assist those who are in the food service business or thinking of joining and want to focus on what it takes to be a successful restaurateur or establishment.

Charles was recognized and chosen as a leader in his role in the provision of African cuisine, to undertake Business Leadership training under the London Development Agency Business leadership training programme in 2008, some of the insights he shares in this book.

Charles is currently registered as a seminar speaker at the London City business library addressing various topics in running a restaurant business. The sample feedback from audience includes: *"Very knowledgeable and able to relay true life experiences. I understood all the aspects that need to be taken into consideration when going into a food business."*

Charles is also registered as a mentor in general and specifically food Businesses with The Idea Trust Charity in London UK. He supports *Business Fights Poverty,* the world's largest community of professional harnessing business for social impact, and believes that creativity and enterprise forging productivity is the best chance of victory in the fight against poverty.